JAPANESE LAYOUT DESIGN

sendp○ints

JAPANESE LAYOUT DESIGN

©2022 Sendpoints Publishing Co., Ltd.
Second printing of the first edition, June 2024

sendpoints

PUBLISHED BY Sendpoints Publishing Co., Ltd.
ADDRESS: Unit 23, L1/F Mirror Tower, 61 Mody Road, Tsim Sha Tsui, Kowloon, Hong Kong, China
PUBLISHER: Lin Gengli
CHIEF EDITOR: Nicole Lo
EXECUTIVE EDITOR: Huang Chujun
ART DIRECTOR: Dongyan Wu
COVER ART DIRECTOR: Daigo Daikoku
COVER DESIGNER: Jianhua Cao
EXECUTIVE ART EDITOR: Peng Zhenwei Design Office
TRANSLATOR: Lin Changfeng
PROOFREADERS: Huang Chujun, Zeng Wanting, Beijing Chinese-Foreign Translation & Information Service Co.,Ltd.   Joseph Taplin

SALES DIRECTOR: Philip Tsang
TEL: +852 6296 2246
EMAIL: sales@sppub.com
WEBSITE: www.sppub.com

ISBN 978-988-76087-8-3

All rights reserved. No part of this publication may be reproduced, stored in a retrieval system or transmitted in any form or by any means, electronic, mechanical, photocopying, recording or otherwise, without prior permission in writing from the publisher. For more information, please contact Sendpoints Publishing Co., Ltd.
Printed and bound in China.

Facebook

Instagram

X

PREFACE

In this era of information explosion, people put more emphasis on effectiveness when performing acts of communication. Conveying information fully and efficiently is crucial for designers, especially graphic designers. Reason and rules have become increasingly central to design, which is usually thought of as a purely artistic process. Even design works that are seemingly random in nature are often the product of rational choices, in which layout design plays an important guiding role.

A system for layouts is the skeleton of graphic design and a must-have in any graphic designer's tool kit. It helps designers organize their ideas and breakthrough fixed mindsets, while also providing solutions to problems. Armed with approaches for layout design, designers can produce visual content that effectively transmits information.

This book introduces Japanese layout design through 6 carefully selected styles from classic Japanese layout designs. These styles are exemplified by over 70 Japanese works of graphic design, including the layouts for magazines, book covers, posters, and advertisements. It analyzes the principles and forms of Japanese design and explores how these works were created. This is a book of inspiration that offers practical approaches for those who want to explore East Asian aesthetics and incorporate them into their works and is suitable for new and experienced designers alike as well as design enthusiasts.

This book was written in hopes that it could provide a good sense of rules and principles to designers and design enthusiasts. It was created to help designers make better graphic design works after embarking on a journey through the excellent design works of Japanese designers who excel at creating something new under the rules presented here.

CONTENTS

Chapter 1 / What's the Big Deal with Layout Design?   008

Chapter 2 / What You Must Know About Japanese Layout Design   014

Chapter 3 / Basic Rules of Japanese Layout Design   018

Chapter 4 / Have You Made These Mistakes?   034

Chapter 5 / Analysis on Japanese Layout Design Works   040

- 01 / High Contrast   **042**
- 02 / Negative Space   **076**
- 03 / Retro Sense   **114**
- 04 / Vividness   **140**
- 05 / Orderliness   **162**
- 06 / Geometric Shapes   **190**

Chapter 6 / Quick Overview of the Layouts in This Book   222

CHAPTER

What's the Big Deal with Layout Design?

- Good layout design conveys information effectively
- Good layout design is a delight to the eyes
- Good layout design tells compelling stories

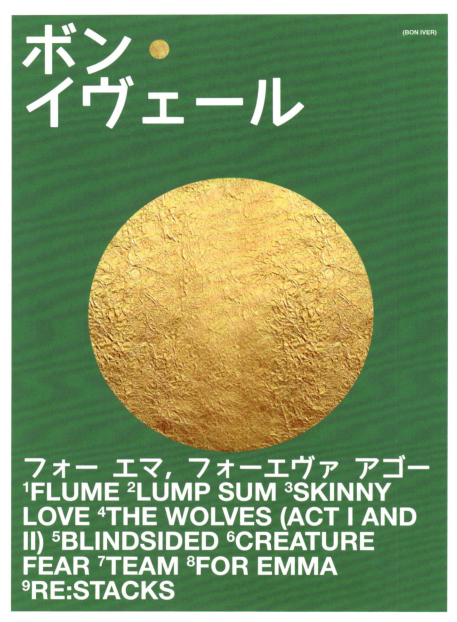

Japanese Posters
Designers: Vitor Manduchi

Layout design involves arrange different elements of a graphic design work. Unlike colors, shapes, or typefaces, layout is something "invisible". It is the skeleton of graphic design, in which various elements are governed by its structure. Good layout design requires not only a good grasp of aesthetics but also rational thinking.

As a tool, layout design can make communication more efficient through visual design. It is a creative process and a combination of reason and aesthetic as well as skill and art. It is also the art of balance. The key of layout design is to leverage goal-oriented thinking to achieve effective visual communication by way of certain skills to select, cut, refine, and rearrange elements such as texts, shapes, colors, and pictures.

When designing a layout, one should also take style into consideration, since layout design is closely related to not only what the information is, but also how it feels to the viewer. A good layout design integrates an excellent arrangement of elements and appropriate style. After a designer has processed and organized information, they should use a certain style and their skills to convey that information effectively.

Broadly speaking, good layout design improves the overall aesthetic sensibility of the design industry and the efficiency of communication among sectors, industries, and communities. Numerous examples in the design world prove the effectiveness of the basic rules for layout design. People are constantly inundated with information, and thus, only content conveyed through a rational and creative design will be noticed, and layout design plays a critical role in making that possible. The communication effect of the same content with different layout approaches will be significantly different.

Japan is one of a few Asian countries that is recognized internationally for its design industry, especially in the area of graphic design. We can learn much from Japan's graphic design, and layout design is an excellent starting point for this as it is the foundation of graphic design and essential if we want to produce good graphic design.

Oftentimes, we can tell that our designs do not look good yet are unable to determine the reason, let alone improve the design. However, if you start the thinking process from the "invisible skeleton" of layout design, you might be discovered by what you find. Layout design is a fundamental course for every designer. If you want to be a good graphic designer, you should first lay a solid foundation, which means having good training in layout design.

A poster promoting the 28th Kamiwasa Award
Designers: Shogo Kizumino and Nozomi Tagami

Good layout design conveys information effectively

Regardless if you are designing the cover of a book or a poster, or mapping out the graphics for product packaging, considering the layout of various elements is a must. There are numerous distinct elements involved in graphic design and various ways to arrange them. Nevertheless, they all follow the basic rules of layout design.

Good layout design enhances the attractiveness of the information presented and increases its understandability. With good layout, the information is separated properly and shown in a form that is easy to comprehend. Texts are classified (through sizing, colors, etc.) and exist in coherence with other elements, such as pictures or graphics.

Good layout design is a delight to the eyes

A designer can arrange elements in many ways, but they should at least aim to make them easy on the eyes and attractive when put together. However, no layout will be perfect for every possible viewer. A designer must weigh pros and cons. For example, a balanced composition is comfortable to look at but also can be dull in appearance. Therefore, before laying out the elements, one should first consider whom and what the design is for and then decide what style is suitable for a given target group. Good layout design is a visual treat, but only for the right viewers.

Good layout design tells compelling stories

We hope that the excellent Japanese layout design works presented in this book will inspire designers and design enthusiasts to explore the possibilities of layout design that is created with fundamental rules. Designers can at times act as messengers between the public and institutions. They rearrange and repackage information, such as an upcoming concert or the story behind a brand, from institutions in visually creative ways and convey it to the public. They use their layout design skills plus other techniques to tell a compelling story.

CHAPTER 2

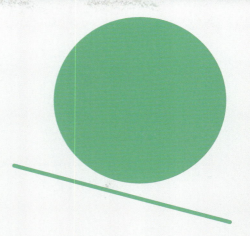

What You Must Know About Japanese Layout Design

- Simplicity
- Emptiness
- Connection of people

Chapter 2 | What You Must Know About Japanese Layout Design

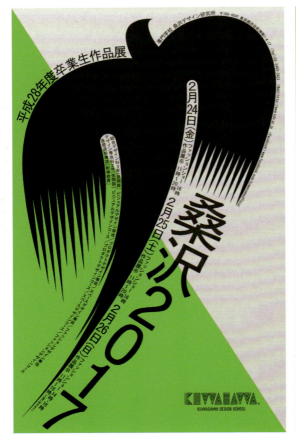
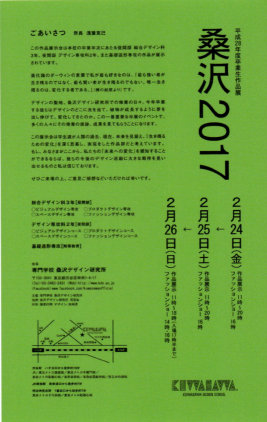

A poster of an exhibition of final year projects of Kuwasawa Design School
Designer: Toru Kase

Simplicity

Clean and simple layouts with limited colors and a prominent focus are what we frequently see in Japanese design. These characteristics originate from Japan's traditional aesthetics. Another key trait, Japan's well-known respect for nature means that they love to use simple elements that are or look natural as a means of constructing things in a simple way.

The Japanese tend to express their perception and feelings for humanity and nature in a simple yet powerful way. Such a way of expression is frequently reflected in Japanese layout design.

Emptiness

Many excellent Japanese design works utilize layouts with limited elements. Japanese graphic designers love to render a subject in a large empty space. The empty space is referred to as "ma" in Japanese, which is often used to describe a specific Japanese concept of negative space. The large negative space encourages viewers to think about endless possibilities. Over time, Japanese aesthetics has undergone a style change. It connects design with life and people, making people yearn for a better life.

Connection of people

A good design connects, catalyzes, and mobilizes the viewer's emotions.

Japanese layout design contains the humanity and caring of Japanese society. Traditionally, the Japanese are humble and restrained. They refrain from expressing their feelings directly. In many cases, they prefer to express themselves or communicate with others in a diplomatic way or use courteous expressions with subtle implications. They follow an unwritten strict code of conduct. In Japan, visual communication design often plays an important role as an intermediary between people and instructions within the context of this highly disciplined society.

● CHAPTER

3

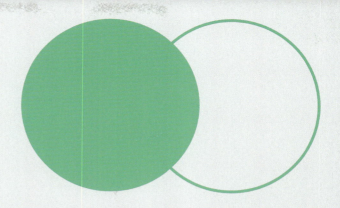

Basic Rules of Japanese Layout Design

- Contrast
- Repetition
- Alignment

● Chapter 3 | Basic Rules of Japanese Layout Design

CONTRAST

Contrast of Colors

Contrast of Spaces ● Contrast of Typography

Contrast of Textures

When to Use Contrast?

Contrast is the most frequently used principle in Japanese layout design. Good contrast attracts the eye and instills intriguing dynamics into a layout.

Creating contrast is arguably the core of layout design that can make a work impressive and allow people to grasp the most important information in a glance. Let's examine how the contrast of the following elements is applied to Japanese layout design.

1. Contrast of Spaces

Creating various contrasting spaces is a critical principle to make your work less dull. Looking closely at graphic design works that have sustainable beauty will reveal that they usually have excellent spatial arrangements that stand up to scrutiny. Contrasting spaces is effective for enhancing focus and improving a design's visual effect as a whole, thus attracting the viewers' interest. Spatial contrast can be created through giving shape to the design's focus or by the contrast between opacity and translucence, or even by creating contrast in terms of distance.

To form a layout with dynamic spaces, be generous in your use of empty spaces. This will allow your work to breathe. Appropriate empty spaces are a very significant element that will make your work easy to look at.

Shape the focus

Opacity vs. Translucence

Contrasting distance

2. Contrast of Typography

Contrast can be formed visually with text, too. Even if you use the same font, you can emphasize a certain part of the text by enlarging or bolding certain letters and numbers.

When words are dense, resizing and bolding are not effective tools for creating contrast. In this case, changing the typeface could be a good option. As a bonus, it may enrich the layout. However, fonts must be chosen carefully based on the information to be presented and the target readers. Contrasts in typography should not damage the integrity and coherence of a layout.

3. Contrast of Colors

Contrast of colors is a regular feature in Japanese layout design. Additionally, the contrast of large background color(s) and focus color(s) in a much lower proportion is also a standard approach that Japanese designers adopt. Besides contrast colors and complementary colors, the contrast of colors can be formed by using different levels of brightness, saturation, and purity of the same color. Such contrast in the same color can be applied to layout design. Of course, the contrast of colors should not be used at the expense of a layout's wholeness and coherence. Contrasting colors should be chosen in light of the work's overall tone.

4. Contrast of Textures

Visually speaking, the texture is the impression created by patterns on the surface. It serves as a symbol that communicates a certain culture or style. A metal or leather texture, for example, might remind people of heavy metal music or an industrial style in interior design, whereas the texture of wood might evoke images of a natural and healthy lifestyle. Textures can vary widely. The contrast between rough and smooth, plain and sophisticated, or visually heavy and light textures enhances an image's expressiveness and thus further stirs the viewer's feelings.

A poster of an event for stray cat adoption
Designer: Dyin Li

Chapter 3 | Basic Rules of Japanese Layout Design

REPETITION

Have you seen any design work that features repetition?

Repetition can be applied to many elements, such as colors and patterns. Repetition of a certain element creates the sense that a work is one interconnected piece. When a series of books is displayed in one visual style, it is the repetition of the style that enhances the connection of the books visually.

Multiple applications of a certain element or a common part of different elements is also a form of repetition. In this way, you can transform a certain element into an iconic sign. Repetition of a common part of different elements creates a more visually impressive look. When an element repeats rhythmically, not only does it make the layout interesting but also establishes a visual order and uniformity.

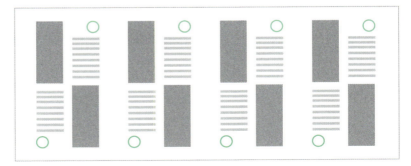

Repetition of a certain element can also serve as a foil for other elements that are the focus of a graphic design work. This allows viewers to take in the subject. It thus can create an order and highlight the subject of a graphic design work.

Sometimes, repetition may also be applied to 2 or more elements to create a visual connection.

Simply repeating one element such as a single picture or pattern does not guarantee the wholeness of a layout, however. Robin Williams, a famous American graphic designer, once noted that techniques for repetition require creating unity through diversity, which is to say that the designer does not rely on one method of repetition alone. At the same time, uniformity in a layout should be maintained.

Repetition conveys a sense of professionalism and authenticity to viewers, especially in printed materials because using the same element is considered to be a design decision.

This Week, a flyer
Designer: Motoi Shito

However, the number of repetitions of an element is not what matters. The importance of the repetition principle lays in how it effects the layout as a whole. Also, how an element repeats is important. A dot in a poster, for example, can reappear somewhere in a different size, color, direction, or distance.

A Japanese poster
Designer: Vitor Manduchi

● Chapter 3 | Basic Rules of Japanese Layout Design

ALIGNMENT

What are visible and invisible alignments for?

The placement of visual elements in the layout of good design work requires a kind of logic. It should strive to convey information in the most appropriate way. Thus, alignment conforms to what viewers are accustomed to consuming visual and is a fundamental technique in layout design. It keeps visual elements in order and determines the connections between those elements.

Main alignment principles:

Left alignment

The most common alignment principle ensures a better reading experience.

Problem: Visual imbalance with more space on the right side.

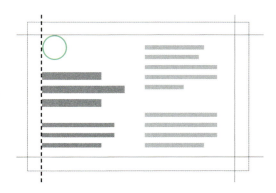

Right alignment

A unique approach but not often used.

Problem: Hard to find the starting point of each line to continue reading.

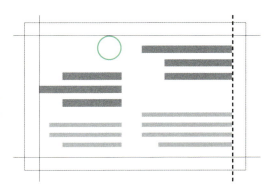

Chapter 3 | Basic Rules of Japanese Layout Design

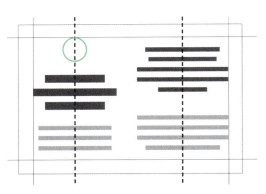

Center alignment

Frequently applied to headlines, leads, and short pieces of texts.

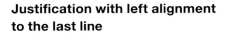

Justification

Neater looking layouts.

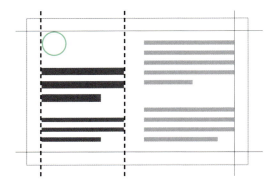

Justification with left alignment to the last line

This leaves no wide space between words at the last line when words on the line are scarce, improving reading efficiency.

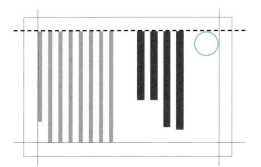

Top alignment

Results in a traditional look for the layout.

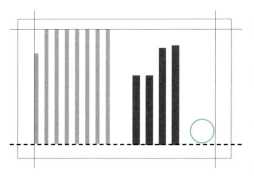

Bottom alignment

Suitable for limited words with a decorative purpose.

Other special alignments

Alignment to an arch

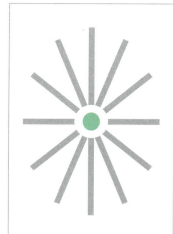

Alignment to a point

Mixed alignment

TIPS:

When a passage is short, left alignment is the proper choice. It creates a random rise and fall on the right side. When a passage is long, justification can make the text look much neater.

Chapter 3 | Basic Rules of Japanese Layout Design

Summary

The 3 principles of layout design (contrast, repetition and alignment) are interconnected. All 3 are necessary for creating good layouts for graphic designs. You have to use 3 of them to achieve the goal of your design. The secret to Japanese layout design is how to mix these principles and break them to create something new. However, before you can break the rules you have to know what they are first. It's only after you grasp the basic skills that you can create new beauty freely with them or even without them.

When we talk about Pablo Picasso, who was famous for his unconventional style, the first thing that comes to our mind is his disfigured portraits. However, we should remember that these artworks were only one part of his long artistic career. He would toss aside a style he developed and then would create a new one once in a few years. However, all of these new styles, such as cubism and surrealism, were based on the solid foundation he had laid at an early age with his sketch skills.

Art and design, as well as other creative fields, share a common trait. That is, free creation is built on top of a good grasp of basic skills, which determine how you can express your idea.

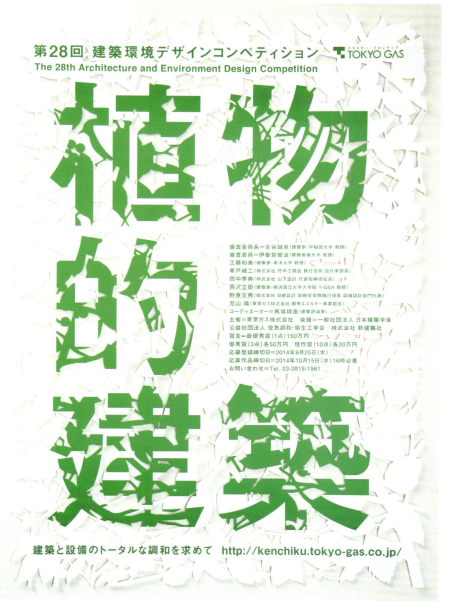

A poster of an architecture and environment competition
Designer: Masayoshi Kodaira

● CHAPTER

4

Have You Made These Mistakes?

- Forgotten about balance and unity
- Lacked clear hierarchy
- Forgotten about the proximity principle

Forgotten about balance and unity

We have discussed alignment, which is usually applied to texts to keep them in a certain order. Other elements in graphic design work also need to be placed in a certain order that makes the layout neat and implies the visual connection among elements.

When the visual elements are grouped and in order, viewers feel comfortable look at them and are able to extract the information easily.

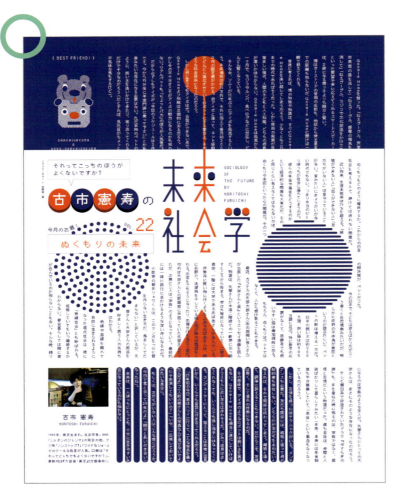

A page of a magazine designed

Designers: Kenjiro Sano and Yumi Katori

On the other hand, when texts are not carefully arranged according to the 3 layout principles, it is hard for viewers to grasp the information and main idea quickly. This is a common mistake. The lack of proper arrangement damages the visual effect and the work's communication function.

TIPS:

Style, design and form ultimately are for the benefit of effectively conveying information. When developing a piece of graphic design work, keep an eye on everything as one unified whole and make sure each visual element is balanced and unified.

Look at the layout below.

Visual elements in it are distant and arranged in no obvious order. Our eyes preferring things to be in order.

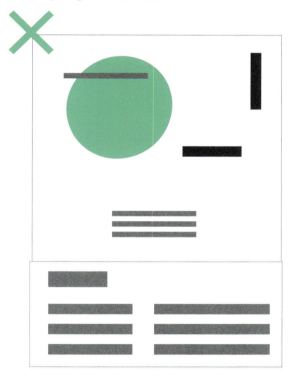

Check those elements to make sure they are connected visually.

Chapter 4 | Have You Made These Mistakes?

Lacked clear hierarchy

Many layouts lack clear distinction and hierarchy among visual elements. Layout design is not only involves making a piece of design work look good, but also includes conveying information effectively. It should help viewers grasp the main idea of the work. A designer should work to make communication happen smoothly from the viewers' perspective.

The text should be arranged in a manner that is consistent with the style of the graphic design's whole composition. In addition, it should be easy for viewers to read and grasp the main point.

A poster for a concert of Geinoh Yamashirogumi, a musical group
Designer: Ryu Mieno

Forgotten about the proximity principle

Similar or related elements should be grouped together?

Which of the 2 layouts below looks better?

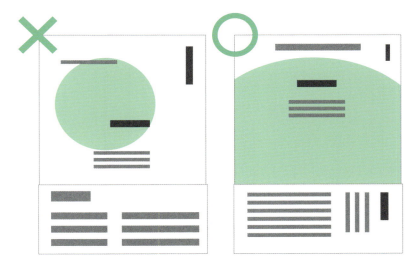

The proximity principle defines how to handle the visual relation of different information. When visual elements are not grouped appropriately, the information in the design work cannot be conveyed effectively and will make viewers uncomfortable.

Applying the proximity principle means grouping similar or related elements. Negative space around grouped visual elements makes the distinction clear.

A designer should first analyze the relationship between the information of different texts before grouping the information and visual elements according to their visual or logical relation. By applying the proximity principle, you can make the layout look organized and neat.

CHAPTER 5

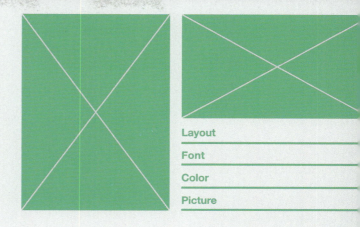

Layout
Font
Color
Picture

Analysis on Japanese Layout Design Works

- 01 ／ High Contrast
- 02 ／ Negative Space
- 03 ／ Retro Sense
- 04 ／ Vividness
- 05 ／ Orderliness
- 06 ／ Geometric Shapes

- Fusion of tradition and modernity
- Eye-catching public transportation posters
- Create movement with shapes derived from a single color
- Enhance the artistic feature of an exhibition with creative fonts
- Bold font doesn't equal a bold poster
- The beauty of cultural heritage reconstructed in a modern way
- A special layout with the subject at the bottom
- Attract attention with a dramatic font
- Different monochrome pictures
- A simple but interesting book cover
- The impressive effect of contrast colors

CHAPTER 5

01

HIGH
CONTRAST

01 FUSION OF TRADITION AND MODERNITY

DESIGNER: Yuri Uenishi

—

They are from a poster series with unique Japanese characteristics that were designed for the 2014 World Team Table Tennis Championships by Yuri Uenishi and renowned artist Taro Yamamoto. Featured in the series is Hanafuda (a Japanese traditional card game) with game scenes to convey the vigor of the table tennis games held in Japan.

> ANALYSIS

Layout

Rather than being focused on the center as is usual, the focus is on the right side. In the foreground, there are well-proportioned elements that are seen as being traditionally Japanese, such as Mount Fuji and the crane. These are contrasted with modern elements, such as a plane and the table tennis net. The border is reminiscent of Hanafuda, a style of Japanese playing cards. All these elements give viewers a fresh, distinctly Japanese impression.

Color

The white background lies low to enhance the contrast between the red and blue.

Font

The dark text stands out from the light background. The golden borders around each letter for "TOKYO" make it look less dull. It also conveys the lofty nobility of Japanese styles.

Picture

The player removed from the original background stands out from the new background in the poster, yet the colors for the subject create a sense of unity between him and the background.

TIPS:

Posters with limited colors deliver a multiple-layered look mainly by variating brightness and saturation. The works here enhance the visual effect through the contrast of warm and cold colors.

FUSION OF TRADITION AND MODERNITY

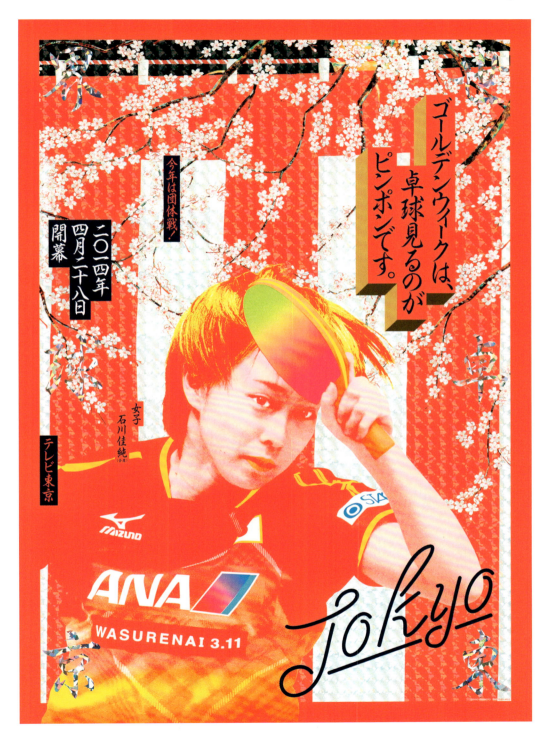

02 EYE-CATCHING PUBLIC TRANSPORTATION POSTERS

Illustrator: Okamura Yuta

They are a series of posters inspired by the Stamp Rally launched by Tokyo Metro to promote good manners on the metro. From April 2017 to March 2018, these posters appeared in every station of the Tokyo Metro, and the topic was changed monthly.

> ANALYSIS

Layout

Each poster is inspired by the concept of what is known as the stamp rally, an activity in Japan where visitors go to different locations to collect stamps. This is a series of concise posters. The yellow ground is very eye-catching, and the illustrations are easy to understand.

Font

Characters with round corners look friendly, boosting the reader's willingness to accept the appealing content.

Color

The posters only feature 3 main colors. The contrast between the sharp yellow and the illustration creates a strong, impressive visual effect.

Picture

The monochrome illustrations in the center of each poster are clean and simple.

EYE-CATCHING PUBLIC TRANSPORTATION POSTERS

03 CREATE MOVEMENT WITH SHAPES DERIVED FROM A SINGLE COLOR

Designer: Yuri Uenishi

A series of posters for the 2015 World Table Tennis Championships.

> ANALYSIS

Layout

"Quick moment" was the subject of posters for the 2015 World Table Tennis Championships. The poster on the left is divided into 2 parts with a line down to the right to create a sense of movement. The 2 lines on the right are evenly divided to give an impression of swiftness yet stillness that is seen in the quick moment of the games.

Color

The large area of blue creates a cool and calm impression, which is balanced by black, a color that is warm but does not create a strong contrast with the blue.

Font

The concise messages with characters and letters in sans-serif types can attract the public's attention.

Picture

The players removed from their original backgrounds are locked in a tense moment. The big contrast between brightness and darkness enhances the dramatic tension.

TIPS:

Different shapes of one color in a certain arrangement can give viewers a visual connection between elements of the design and perception of the physical space. These posters successfully create a sense of depth through the contrast between brightness and darkness, especially the shadows. These posters feature carefully arranged elements that are detailed and artistic.

1. Hollowing out

2. Dots

3. Flowing

4. Texture

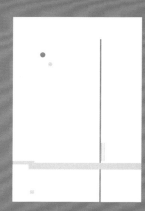

5. Plan

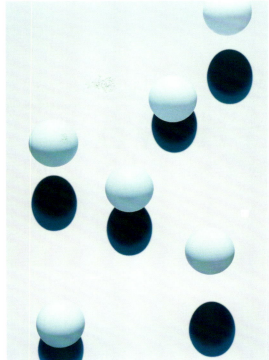

04 ENHANCE THE ARTISTIC FEATURE OF AN EXHIBITION WITH CREATIVE FONTS

Designer: Masayoshi Kodaira

The logo for Art Fair Tokyo launched in 2005 was designed by the designer who is still designing posters for the event. The dominant colors used are typically silver or golden. After some changes were made to the fair in 2015, Kodaira tried to express his expectation of a bright future ahead when designing the posters. He was also engaged in the designing process for the fair's venue as well as the lighting for concerts held during the fair.

> ANALYSIS ① The creative combination of kanji and English letters 056/057

Layout

The whole poster is stuffed with Japanese characters, providing an abundance of information. Though the words are dense, kerning and line spacing make the content easy and comfortable to read. The combination of "Art Fair Tokyo" and the kanji for "Tokyo" is very creative.

Font

The sans-serif kanji and English letters are presented in the same style. Though some parts of the kanji are replaced by English words, they remain recognizable. The balanced composition of the 2 kanji enhances the impression of the design's stability.

Color

The matching of black and red is classic. The black words in the background offer a certain sense of steadiness.

② **Artistic black and white**

> ANALYSIS

Layout

The poster is equally divided into 3 parts. A picture of a Tokyo street scene is filled in with kanji and English words.

Font

The combination of the street scene and the words stand out.

Color

The black-and-white create a sense of calm.

Picture

Even with the combination of the picture and words, the street scene is still clear, and the words are legible. The way the designer created is impressive.

> ANALYSIS

③ **Attract viewers with a culture icon**

Layout

This is a balanced poster that has been equally divided into 3 parts. Words and cherry blossoms, a cultural icon of Japan, are blended creatively.

Font

The combination of the picture and multi-language words is stylish and also very impressive.

Picture

The fresh and bright flowers, which are placed on a background with low saturation, make the poster look bright but not difficult to view.

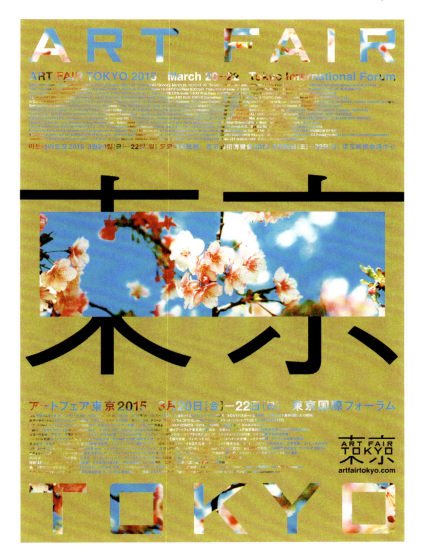

05 BOLD FONT DOESN'T EQUAL A BOLD POSTER

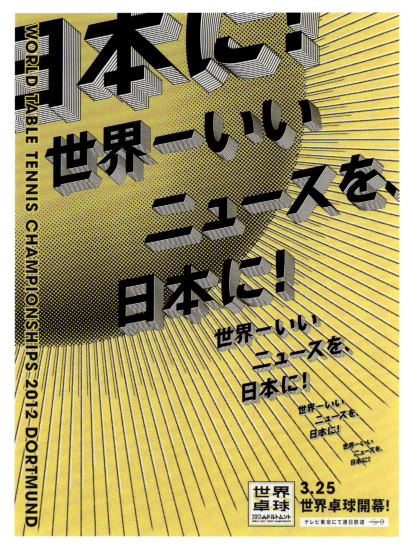

Designer: Yuri Uenishi

—

A series of posters for the 2012 World Table Tennis Championships.

Font
The 3D font brings out the characters, making the posters look confrontational.

Layout
With the radial lines around the table tennis ball, the designer visualizes the threatening and speedy ball, reminding viewers of the tension during the table tennis games.

Color
The main visual elements are in black atop a yellow background. Lines in different densities create a sense of multiple physical spaces, and they have a distinct look, reminding viewers of manga, a unique form of Japanese visual culture.

TIPS:
Forms and layers in posters with monochromatic visual elements are constructed with shades and changes in color saturation or the densities of various lines and dots. The elements in these posters here are formed using different shades, which are illusions made of lines and dots of varying densities.

06 THE BEAUTY OF CULTURAL HERITAGE RECONSTRUCTED IN A MODERN WAY

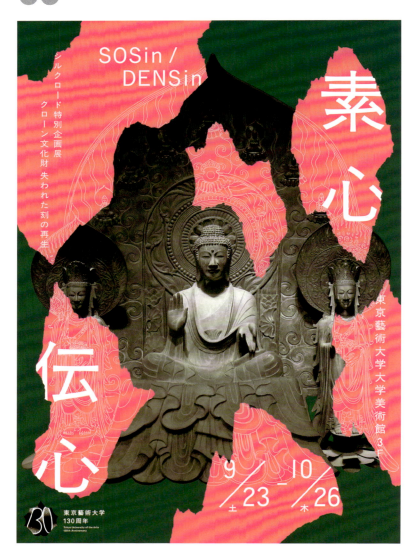

Designers: Masashi Murakami and Moe Shibata
Studio: Emuni

The exhibition posters were for the 130th anniversary of the Tokyo University of the Arts by Murakami and Shibata, who also were the art directors of the exhibition. This exhibition features "clone cultural property". The images or outlines of the disappearing and vanished relics were reproduced with advanced imaging technology, thus blending traditional arts and crafts with modern technology and aesthetics.

> ANALYSIS

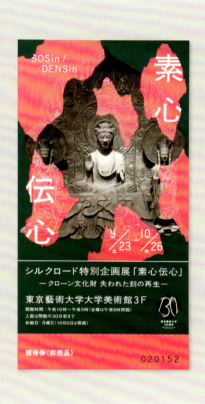
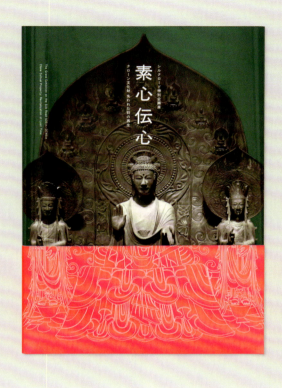

Layout

The contrast of a sharp and modern peach color and the ancient carving reflects the notion of recreating Japan's cultural heritage.

Font

The characters of the theme are in the peach section. This layout allows the viewer to obtain the necessary information at a glance.

Color

Bright peach areas create an attractive look, whereas the gray subject and shady green background create a sense of stillness.

Picture

The elegant curves of the carving contrast the irregular outlines of the peach sections.

07 A SPECIAL LAYOUT WITH THE SUBJECT AT THE BOTTOM

> ANALYSIS

Layout
The focus, the monochrome figure, is on the bottom of the book cover. This approach breaks the mold of the typical layout. Above the figure are sections of various colors, which form a striking contrast between the black and white figure.

Font
The loose and sloppy words create a whimsical feeling.

Color
The translucent colors on the background of the picture help bring out the figure without drawing away from the detail of the picture.

Picture
The contrast between the color zones and the monochrome figure is fascinating.

Designer: Hiroshi Hino

The cover of a book by Jinichi Uekusa, a film critic.

いつも夢中になったり飽きてしまったり

植草甚一

08 ATTRACT ATTENTION WITH A DRAMATIC FONT

> ## ANALYSIS

Layout
The designer Ryu Mieno focused his effort on creating an impressive font to attract the viewers' attention to the theme of the poster. Creating dramatic fonts is his favorite approach to draw people to his content.

Font
The words rendered in a creative font by Mieno are intertwined and well-matched with the theme of the exhibition.

Color
This uses only 2 colors for a simple and retro look.

Designer: Ryu Mieno

It is a poster for an exhibition "Operating Contacts" curated by Ryu Mieno. The artworks of Kohei Takahashi and Ryu Mieno, as well as the other 4 artists, were displayed during the exhibition.

09 A POSTER WITH DENSE STRAIGHT LINES

> ANALYSIS

Layout

The dense straight lines across the words create a structured but tense impression. Some lines do not run parallel to the vertical, horizontal, or 45-degree lines creating a more dynamic look.

Font

The strokes of the red letters are basically parallel to the vertical and horizontal lines, adding a much structured feeling to this vigorous font.

Color

The red color and its contrast with the green background create a strong visual impression.

Designer: Ryu Mieno

–

In 2016, LLC Insects of *IN/SECTS* magazine threw an event "KITAKAGAYA FLEA & ASIA BOOK MARKET" that gathered people engaged in food, art, design, literature, etc. to celebrate the 10th anniversary of the magazine.

10 DIFFERENTIATE BOOKS OF A SERIES WITH DIFFERENT MONOCHROME PICTURES

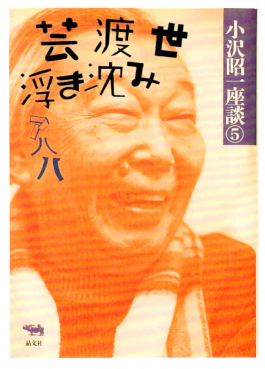

> ANALYSIS

Layout
Each book cover is a picture of a figure with a strongly appealing expression that fully expresses the characteristics of the theme.

Font
The loose and unaligned characters are like hand-cut for a cute and visually friendly look.

Color
Done in a particular color, the pictures reflect the tone of each book. When the books are put together, the colors are well matched.

Picture
Each book's cover is fully occupied by the picture to make the figure more impactful.

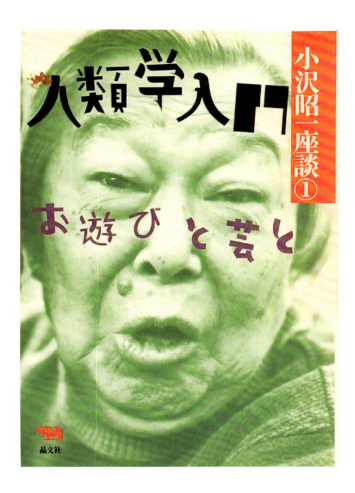

Designer: Kouga Hirano

The covers of books by Shoichi Ozawa.

11 A SIMPLE BUT INTERESTING BOOK COVER

Designer: Hiroko Sakai

The cover of the book on design included a case study, titled "Key Visuals for Design Development: Promoting Ideas That Win the Eye".

> ANALYSIS

Layout

The cover is divided into 2 equal parts in different colors. Using simple lines and circles, the designer expresses the theme of the book and expands on the original idea.

Font

A strong sense of contrast is created through cold and warm colors.

Color

There are 6 main sections in 4 colors. The circles are in the same colors as the rectangles. In this way, the circles echo the title in the rectangles in a visually striking way. At the same time, the design maintains the balance and unity of the colors.

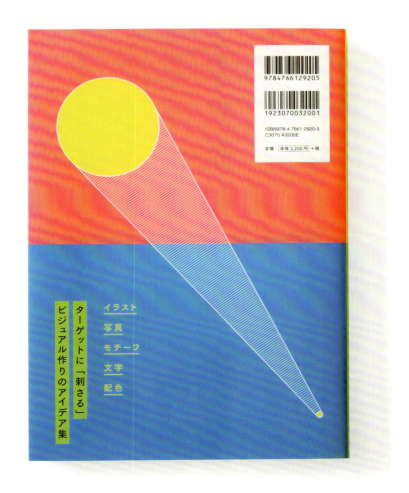

TIPS:

The contrast of cold and warm colors creates a visual impact on the viewers.

A SIMPLE BUT INTERESTING BOOK COVER

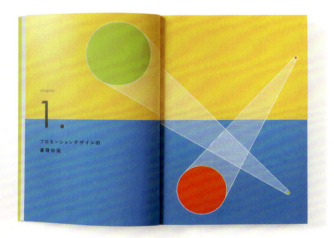

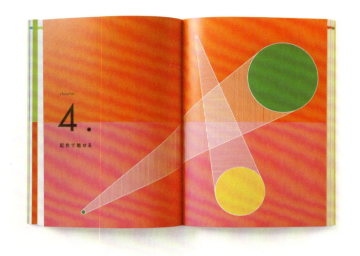

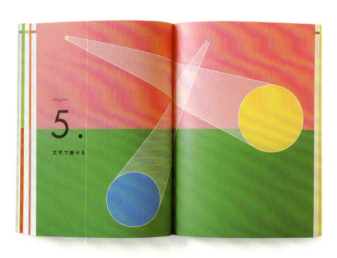

12 THE IMPRESSIVE EFFECT OF CONTRAST COLORS

Designer: Toru Kase

This book introduces fantasy bookstores in Japan. On the back of the book, it states that the books mentioned do not exist.

> ANALYSIS

Layout
Characters are aligned to strange curve lines to imply the subject of the book – the bookstores of fantasy. The colors and composition echo the book.

Color
The orange and blue are contrast colors, creating a strong visual impact together.

Font
Since the book is a collection of stories written by several authors, the designer chose MS Gothic and Soft Gothic that are frequently used in Japanese guide books.

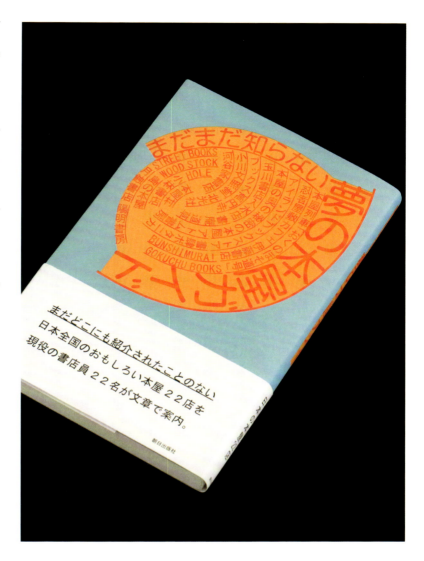

TIPS: Complementary Color vs. Contrasting Color
A pair of complementary colors are on the opposite side of the color wheel, which creates strong contrast when they are put next to each other. While the contrasting colors of a certain color are a range of colors 90 degrees to the left and right of the complementary color on the wheel, such as red and yellow that are contrasting colors of blue. The juxtaposition of such colors creates a mild contrasting feeling.

● Fresh

Japanese impressions formed with color gradients

／● Exquisite tour brochure ／● Monochromatic but multi-layered ／

● Highlight the main visual elements using negative space ／● A tension formed

by aligning words at a diagonal ／● Warning presented in a gentle but strong way ／

● A book on a poster or a poster of a book ／● Communicate the message with ease and

accuracy ／● Posters with a pet theme ／● Simple illustration with large negative space ／

● Convey the charm of art installations ／● A cover design full of deep feelings ／● A

clean and delightful cover ／● A calendar that gives you a sense of ritual ／

● Express the real meaning of the words with vivid movements ／

● Creating posters with social impact

CHAPTER 5

02

NEGATIVE SPACE

13 FRESH JAPANESE IMPRESSIONS FORMED WITH COLOR GRADIENTS

Studio: Luck Show

—
It is part of a visual project for a themed hall named "Citizen Cooperation for Disaster Reduction" at the UN World Conference on Disaster Risk Reduction. The design studio Luck Show also designed a series of special towels and other objects to create the image of the hall where people discussed how to prevent disasters.

> ANALYSIS

Layout

The subject is a circle that has 2 colors gradually blending in a balanced composition. It creates a cozy impression in a classic Japanese style.

Font

The words are neatly placed in a justified alignment. The thin strokes are made in a handwritten style creating a light feeling.

Color

The contrast of blue and yellow is weakened by their light hues to enhance the layering and elevate the image's artistry for a quintessential Japanese style.

TIPS:

Gradually changing between 2 contrasting colors does not wipe out the contrast entirely but rather makes it mild. The brightness and purity of the colors achieve an overall unity in vision.

FRESH JAPANESE IMPRESSIONS FORMED WITH COLOR GRADIENTS

14 EXQUISITE TOUR BROCHURE

Designer: Daigo Daikoku
Studio: Daikoku Design Institute

A visual project for a Buddhist ceremony that was held when the reconstruction of the renowned Three-Story Pagoda in Chinzanso Garden was completed.

> ANALYSIS

Layout

A good number of visual elements here, such as the outlines and layout of the pagoda, are designed to present the characteristics of the three-story pagoda.

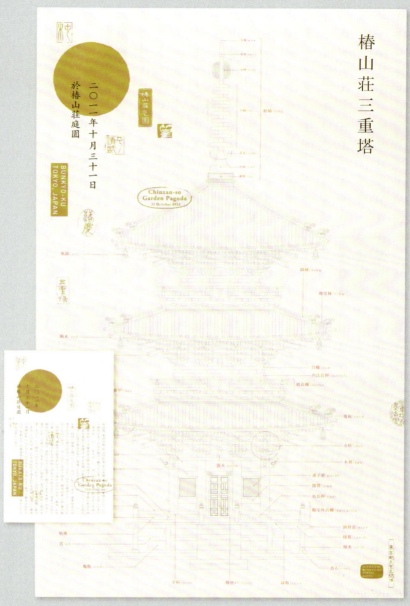

15 MONOCHROMATIC BUT MULTI-LAYERED

Designers: Shogo Kizumino and Nozomi Tagami

The poster, flyer, and envelope for the 28th Kamiwasa Award. Kamiwasa is the Japanese term for papercraft. The white patterns employed serve as a collection of some basic aspects of papercraft design.

> ANALYSIS

Layout

The poster, flyer, and envelope are in black and white but feature a variety of shades, forms and layers. This is the interesting part of the posters. Shading plays an important role in this work, with the patterns for the shading inspiring creative flights of fancy.

Font

Some Japanese characters are cut along the outlines of the patterns to enhance the image of traditional papercrafts and increase the poster's layered look.

Color

The poster, flyer, and envelope are done in black-and-white, but the shading and details create a multiple-layered effect and help to present the theme visually.

16 HIGHLIGHT THE MAIN VISUAL ELEMENTS USING NEGATIVE SPACE

Designer: Agata Yamaguchi

A poster of Yamakuchi fishing bait shop that utilizes the brand's marker, the sakana pattern.

> ANALYSIS

Layout

The subject of the black-and-white poster is the same 6 patterns in different sizes. The patterns are deformations of " 魚 " (sakana), a kanji that means fish. The sizes and arrangement of the patterns create an impression of space. The sakana patterns neatly convey the nature of the brand and its product.

Font

The sakana patterns allow viewers to quickly surmise what products are being advertised. Although the kanji has been deformed, it is still recognizable by viewers.

Color

Monochromatic posters are frequently seen in Japan.

TIPS:

Tips for arranging visual elements in a layout: 1. Create differences between visual elements; 2. Each individual element must be done well enough; 3. Elements should be of different sizes; 4. Spacing between elements is to be elaborately calculated; 5. Create the illusion of space between elements.

HIGHLIGHT THE MAIN VISUAL ELEMENTS USING NEGATIVE SPACE

17 A TENSION FORMED BY ALIGNING WORDS AT A DIAGONAL

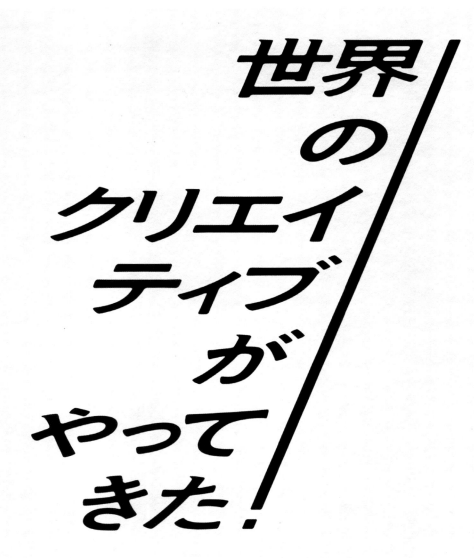

> ANALYSIS

Layout

When words are placed diagonally, they create a falling visual, which conveys a sense of tension to the viewer.

Font

The italic text enhances the tension further.

Designer: Keita Asaoka

–

The designer expressed the shock he felt about the creative artwork the Tokyo National Museum collected from around the world. The designer conveyed this feeling of shock by using visually falling words and the exclamation mark – the long slant line with a dot below it.

A TENSION FORMED BY ALIGNING WORDS AT A DIAGONAL

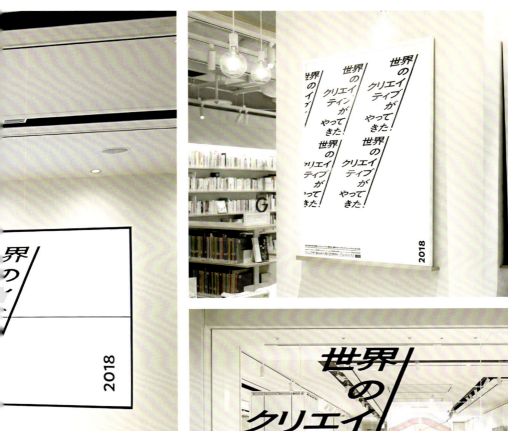

18 WARNING PRESENTED IN A GENTLE BUT STRONG WAY

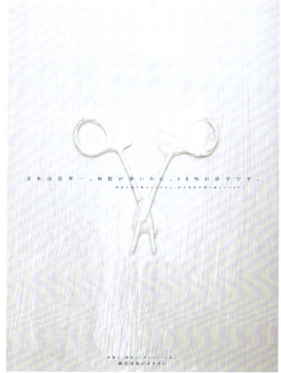

Designer: Daisaku Ono
Studio: Creative Company GIFT

—

A series of posters for Leoclan, a consulting firm specializing in healthcare facility management. Medical tools are covered with white paint, warning the medical institutions that mismanagement could lead to medical incidents.

> ANALYSIS

Layout

Almost completely white posters with certain shades of gray blend medical tools with the background to create a gentle but strong feeling to viewers.

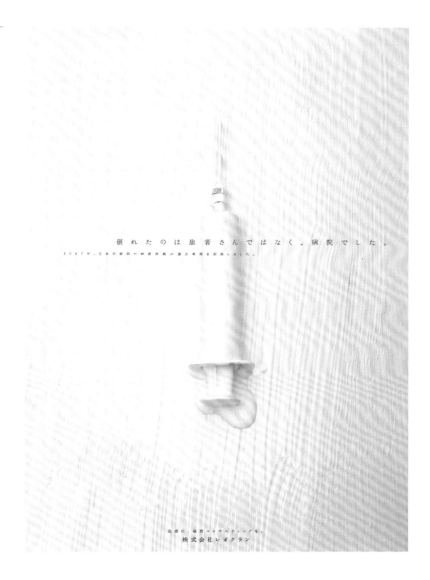

19 A BOOK ON A POSTER OR A POSTER OF A BOOK

> ANALYSIS

Layout
The balanced composition creates a sense of calm and confidence. The text is concise and eye-catching. What's so interesting about this poster of a book is that it looks like a book on a poster.

Font
The classic serif font of the Japanese text produces a classic yet mysterious look.

BRUTUS, Issue 838
Chief Editor: Zenta Nishita

A well-known Japanese lifestyle magazine. This is a special edition themed "Dangerous Reading" that introduced books and shared the joy of reading.

COMMUNICATE THE MESSAGE WITH EASE AND ACCURACY

> ANALYSIS

Layout

The subject in the middle is prominent, while the title is sharp and bright.

Color

The colors for different elements echo each other with their contrast and similarity. The yellow laid out on cold background colors is prominent and creates a touch of vividness that is a foil for the crisp light blue and white.

BRUTUS, Issue 842

With the theme "New Wave of Tea", this issue features articles on tea balls from around the world and explores the development of the tea ball design.

21 POSTERS WITH A PET THEME

> ANALYSIS

Layout
The posters' subjects are displayed toward the bottom, which makes the cat paintings an visual center. The design produces a retro and mild vibe.

Font
The English words are rendered in a traditional calligraphy style.

Color
The low-value colors generate a sense of simplicity.

Picture
The style of cat paintings is consistent with the traditional font.

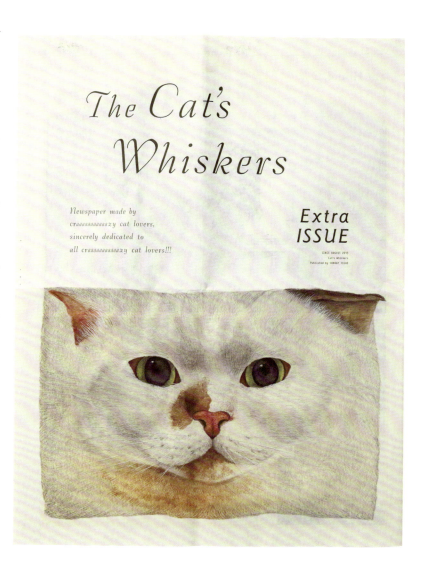

Designer: Ken Okamoto

—
The Cat's ISSUE project gathered artists and designers to share their love of cats. They held an exhibition on cats, published *The Cat's Whiskers* magazine, and sold their cat-related products in pop-up stores. Part of the generated revenue was directed toward campaigns to help cats.

22 SIMPLE ILLUSTRATION WITH LARGE NEGATIVE SPACE

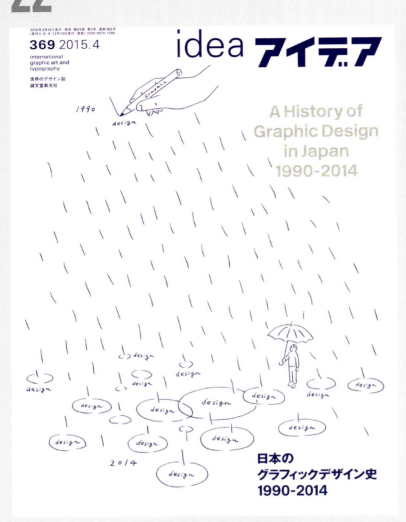

> ANALYSIS

Layout
The magazine cover is an illustration made up of only lines in one color, which hints at the connection between today's graphic design and that design of the 1990s.

Font
Sans-serif font matches the simple illustration well.

Color
The simple illustration in white and light blue lightens up the subject matter.

idea, Issue 369
Chief Editor: Kiyonori Muroga

idea is one of the most influential and credible design magazines in Japan. The cover story for this issue was on the history of Japanese design from 1990 to 2014.

23 CONVEY THE CHARM OF ART INSTALLATIONS

> ANALYSIS

Layout

Daijiro Ohara formed 2 characters " 曲线 " (kyokushin) with electric wires and conductor cables before a deep blue background. In this way, it attracts the eyes to the subject. The first character could mean either "curved" or "song", while the second character means "line". Thus, it can be translated as curved lines or "song lines".

Color

The deep blue makes the black and white wires more prominent.

Picture

The "curved line" made up of wires is a brilliant way to express the theme.

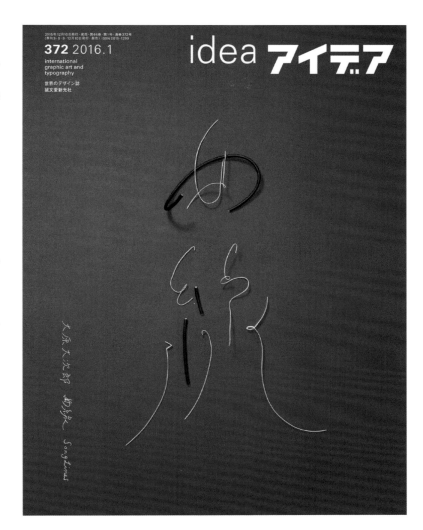

***idea*, Issue 372**

—
The main content of this issue is the "Curved Lines" of Daijiro Ohara.

24 A COVER DESIGN FULL OF DEEP FEELINGS

> ANALYSIS

Layout

This layout makes the overall look clean and intuitive. The designer created a font that expresses a strong personal feeling.

Font

The lower part of the first black character in the title appears to be a strong arm, while the upper part of the second black character is like a sturdy roof.

Color

The dark colors of the words create a sense of stability.

Designer: Koga Hirano

The book cover of *Lao She: the Father of Beijing*. The passion for designing the book covers for the writers and poets he loved is something special, Hirano said. The characters " 老舍 " (Lao She) are his favorite.

25 A CLEAN AND DELIGHTFUL COVER

> ANALYSIS

Layout
A minimal cover formed with characters in boxes that become increasingly smaller from left to right and top to bottom.

Color
The magenta is delightful addition to the blue and black.

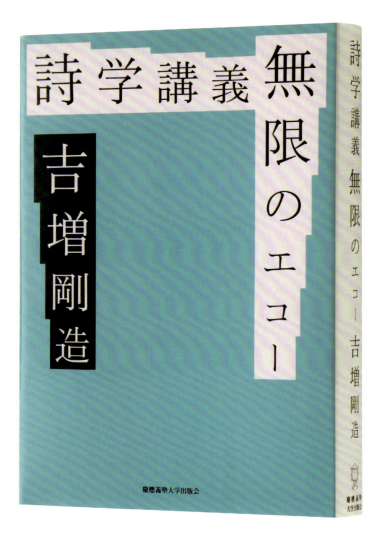

Designer: Kazunari Hattori

A book cover.

26 A CALENDAR THAT GIVES YOU A SENSE OF RITUAL

Designer: Yoshinaka Ono

—
A calendar with an italic font in a handwritten style.

> ANALYSIS

Layout

Additional parts of the calendar can be flipped to create a sense of ritual for daily life.

Font

The words and numbers in a handwritten style provide the calendar with a personal touch.

27 EXPRESS THE REAL MEANING OF THE WORDS WITH VIVID MOVEMENTS

Designer: Yeongmin Won

Yeongmin Won attempted to bring life to words through the dynamics of the human body. She believed that language as a means of expression was not enough to represent human behavior. Writing the word "run" on the skin does not allow you to feel the action of running. Rather, it is only by actually running can we feel the movement of the muscles. In this series of posters, Won tried to convey a "3-dimensional truth" (or the instant feeling words give you) or perhaps "the truth of the truth". She believed that this approach would lead people to engage in a real life, which brims with energy and vitality.

> ANALYSIS

Layout
Only one bright color at the center of each poster attracts viewers to the information being conveyed and expresses the designer's creative tension.

Font
The minimal font enhances the vividness of the poster.

Color
The fresh and delightful cyan blends well with the spirit the poster conveyed.

EXPRESS THE REAL MEANING OF THE WORDS WITH VIVID MOVEMENTS

CREATING POSTERS WITH SOCIAL IMPACT

> ANALYSIS

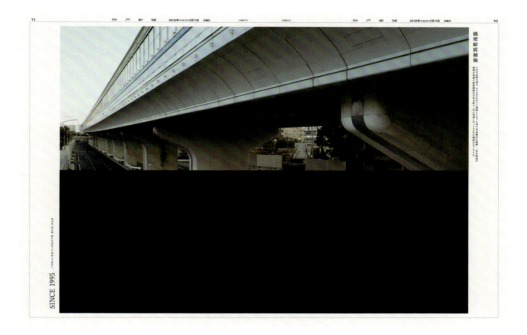

Layout

The layout has the appearance of a newspaper. The contrast between the emotionally restrained photo and the large black block creates a unique vibe and gives ample room for imagination.

Picture

The pictures are familiar urban scenes after an area has recovered from an earthquake, giving viewers a warm and friendly feeling.

Designer: Yoshinaka Ono

This was a special project led by Kobe Newspaper to review the Great Hanshin Earthquake in 1995. In the upper and lower parts of the posters, a comparison is made between the present after reconstruction and the time of the earthquake. The upper part of each poster is a picture of what people built before 1995 with a description of it on the right. The lower part is a black box with "SINCE 1995", expressing the impact of the earthquake and the lack of countermeasures. The purpose of this project was to make people reflect on the earthquake not only with sadness but also with pride in the achievements of the Japanese people after the tragedy. It also encourages people to turn that pride into motivation for moving forward.

CREATING POSTERS WITH SOCIAL IMPACT

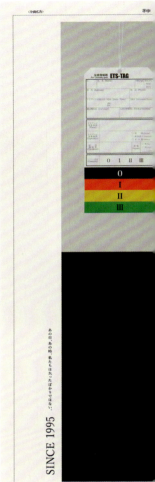

トリアージ

大災害の直後は多数の傷病者が発生する。そこで救える命を優先的に救うために緊急な治療を要する患者を瞬時に見つけることが重要。日本では阪神・淡路大震災以後、定着した。

みんなの家

神戸市西区にみんなが共同で集まるコミュニティハウスのこと。阪神・淡路大震災で、家族や住居を失った高齢者が住んだ「ふれあい住宅」が日本での最初の例ともされる。

SINCE 1995

あの日、あの時、私たちは失ったばかりではない…

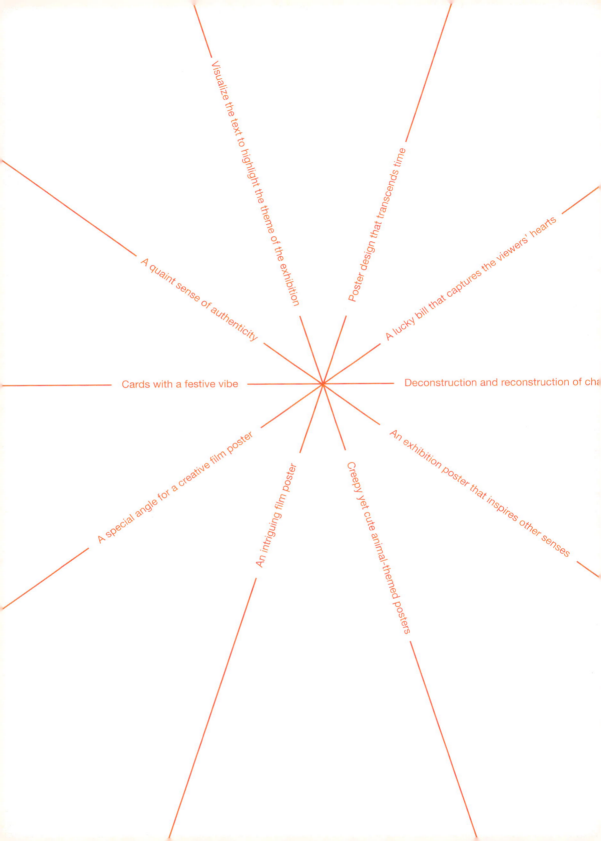

CHAPTER 5

RETRO
SENSE

29 DECONSTRUCTION AND RECONSTRUCTION OF CHARACTERS

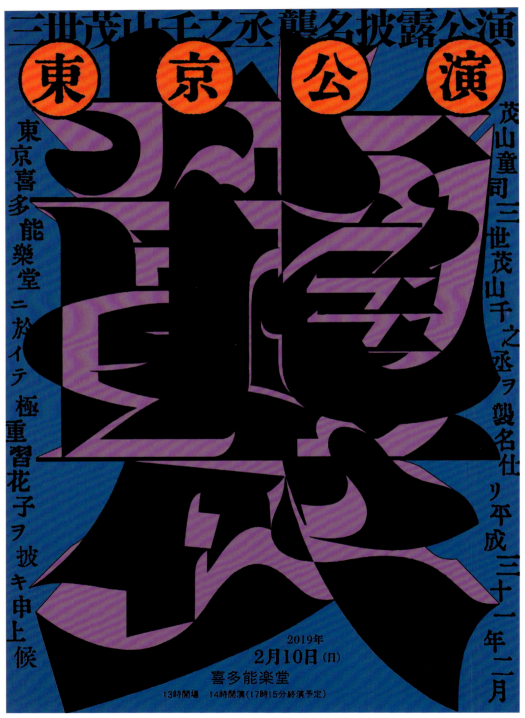

> ANALYSIS

Layout
The creative characters occupy most of the poster area and generate a strong visual impact.

Font
The big characters constructed with stylish strokes are powerful.

Color
The retro colors go well with the style of the concert.

Designer: Ryu Mieno

—
Posters for a concert.

POSTER DESIGN THAT TRANSCENDS TIME

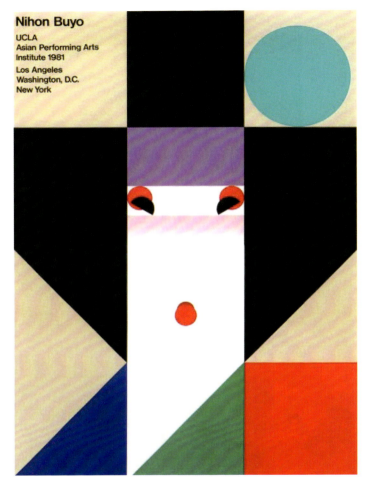

> ANALYSIS

Layout

Simple patterns in perfect proportion form the image of a geisha, a typical symbol of Japanese culture. This impressive work was groundbreaking in the 1980s.

Color

The lively colors give the poster a very delightful touch.

Designer: Ikko Takana

Kazumitsu Tanaka, one of Japan's leading graphic designers, is represented by posters for a Japanese dance performance in 1981. The posters fuse modernism principles and aesthetics with traditional Japanese elements, and they create an international visual effect.

31 A LUCKY BILL THAT CAPTURES THE VIEWERS' HEARTS

> ANALYSIS

Layout
A balanced layout with rich and abundant elements.

Font
The characters in the middle of the front side are done in the official script for a retro touch.

Color
The light yellow and green make the lucky bill appear both antique and elegant.

Designer: Koji Ohhigashi
Studio: AD FAHREN

This bill is part of the packaging for " ぶどう饅頭 " (grape buns). Grape bun is a very popular grape-like snack in Tokushima Prefecture, Japan, with a history of over 100 years. This explains why grapes are featured so prominently. There is no 100-million-yen bill in Japan. The astronomical figure is to express the impact on the person who receives it. It is said that if dreams and wishes are written on the ticket, they will come true. This belief has led to the ticket becoming very popular in Japan as a symbol of luck.

32 VISUALIZE THE TEXT TO HIGHLIGHT THE THEME OF THE EXHIBITION

> ANALYSIS

Layout

It is impressive and important to convey the meaning of the text and the theme of the exhibition – changing – with the symbolic and liquid-shaped words.

Font

The liquid nature of the font emphasizes that flowing and changing nature of the subject.

Color

The neon color acts as a foil for the blue-gray background.

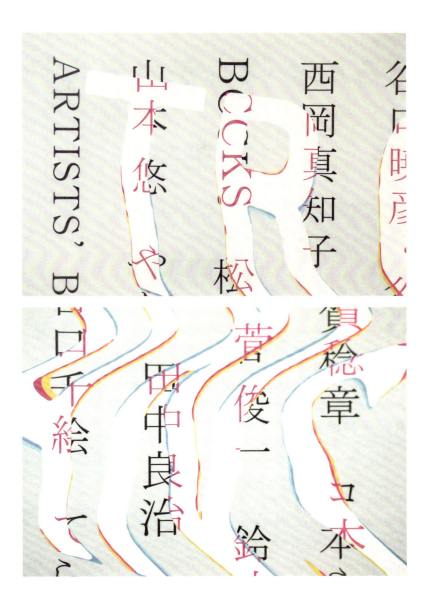

Designer: Yurie Hata

A poster for Trans Books, an exhibition on the future of books.

33   A QUAINT SENSE OF AUTHENTICITY

Studio: Taku Satoh Design Office Inc.

This series of posters is the visual design of the Japanese Kihin orange brand. The word "Kihin" stands for the best quality of the kumquat brand in Japan. The designer's branding design takes into account the brand's appeal in terms of the taste and unique sweetness of its oranges. The design also captures how the brand comes from a prestigious production area. The overall design is simple, retro, and powerful.

> ANALYSIS

Layout

Pictures of the same scene at different angles were cut and laid out in the posters to form a connection between each poster. The poster series is a good example of telling a brand story through pictures.

34 CARDS WITH A FESTIVE VIBE

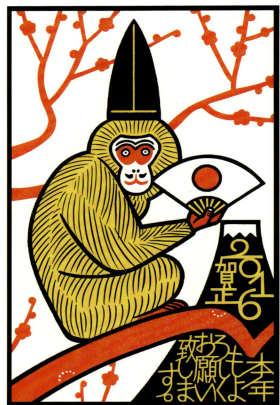

Studio: Studio-Takeuma

A series of 12 zodiacs cards, celebrating New Year's Day.

> ANALYSIS

Layout
Rich in traditional features, the visual elements in the cards are interlaced and layered in an interesting style.

Font
The creative fonts of the characters go well with other visual elements.

Color
The colors are vivid but not loud, giving a strong traditional and festive vibe.

35 A SPECIAL ANGLE FOR A CREATIVE FILM POSTER

> ANALYSIS

Layout
The background of the poster is essentially a pun, being either an image of a grassland or the fur of Totoro, a big cat-like creature from the animated film. The 2 girls thus appear to be searching for Totoro yet are simultanouesly surrounded by the cute creature thanks to this visual perspective.

Font
The title of the film – the most important information – is in a stylized font and is done in the same shade of green as the hair or grass. Other words are small and concise in order to maintain the impact of the drawing.

Color
The designer changed the color of Totoro to be a grassy green, which is a warm tone that matches the theme nicely.

TIPS:
When designing a film poster, a designer should understand the core of the film and express that core through a unique visual form. Thus, the designer should have a good insight into the film from a different angle and then find a creative way to express it.

Designer: Huang Hai

The poster for *Totoro* by Zhuye, a Chinese film poster design company. This well-known cartoon icon is overflowing with the nostalgia of a happy childhood, causing the viewer to have a strong desire to hug Totoro.

36 AN INTRIGUING FILM POSTER

> ANALYSIS

Layout

This special poster is in a classic ukiyo-e style, with waves to remind viewers of The Great Wave off Kanagawa, the best-known painting of this genre. The joyful people under an umbrella playing with the waves in the center draw the viewer's curiosity.

Font

The title of the film is done in a handwritten style and located at the bottom right of the poster, completing the overall image. The transparent box for the title blends with the painting while also highlighting it.

Color

The woodcut style for the faded picture creates a retro vibe.

Designer: Huang Hai

A poster for promoting *Shoplifters* in China. It is a film directed by Hirokazu Koreeda about a non-biological family coping with a life of poverty.

37 CREEPY YET CUTE ANIMAL-THEMED POSTERS

Designer: Kazuaki Horitomo Kitamura

Monmon Cats by Kazuaki Horitomo Kitamura was inspired by tattoos and cats, both of which he adored. Monmon is the romanization of a Japanese word that means tattoo.

> ANALYSIS

Layout

Japan's tattoo culture is incorporated to create a chic and unconventional style.

Color

Colors frequently used in traditional Japanese artwork produce a retro vibe.

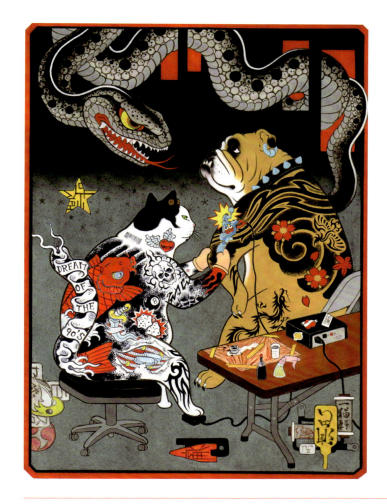

TIPS:

Pay attention to the roles of a picture in a layout:

 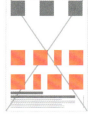 

1. the focus;   2. the background;   3. the support in the corner.

When adding text to a picture, avoid damaging the overall feeling of the picture.

38 AN EXHIBITION POSTER THAT INSPIRES OTHER SENSES

> ## ANALYSIS

Layout
The theme of the exhibition is "Open Storage: Crispy Storage / Creamy Room". The overall layout of the exhibition is out of the ordinary and features bold colors. The designer used stacked chocolate, fruits, and sweets for creative thematic imagery. The taste of "rich" and "crispy" is cross-linked with visual images and builds one each other to produce semantic meaning. This playful mix showcases the essence of the exhibition and provides a memorable sensory experience for viewers.

Font
The text for the layout creates an overcrowding feeling to communicate the richness and surprise of this warehouse exhibition: a multi-sensory delight for visitors.

Color
The poster makes full use of the associative effect of colors. The combination of irregular pink patterns and the black-and-white background and text creates a contrast between lightness and boldness, mirroring the exhibition's theme that large-scale artworks can also bring subtle and delightful multi-sensory inspiration.

Picture
The images are displayed as a collage in a surreal style, using a clever flexible design language for a transcendent scene that creates an experiential visual effect.

Designer: Ryu Mieno

A poster for the 4th "Open Storage" exhibition hosted by Chidori Bunka in MASK (Mega Art Storage Kitakagaya). Artworks by Teppei Kaneuji, Muneteru Ujino, Hironari Kubota, Kohei Nowa were showcased during the exhibition.

39   GIVE A SPECIAL MOMENT BETWEEN CHAPTERS

Designer: Yoshimaru Takashi

Nostalgic Printed Matter Museum of the Family (or Retoro na Insatsubutsu Gokazoku no Hakubutsu-shi) is a book by Yoshimaru Takashi. He gathered print matter from Japanese products since the 20th century. The book is divided according to generation, gender and the consumer, with customers being seen as "family member".

> ANALYSIS

Layout

The 2 pages are a simple juxtaposition of a drawing and simple text, providing a breathing space for readers to both take in and add something special to the book.

Font

The fonts and the drawings of the family members were all created by the designer. The kanji are written in a simplified way while maintaining their clarity and readability.

40 A CLASSY BOOK COVER IN A TRADITIONAL STYLE

> ANALYSIS

Layout

Japanese text traditionally runs from top to bottom and from right to left. The book cover, too, follows this convention. The placement of the 2 drawings follows the same order.

Font

The font created by the designer is unique in its creativity yet retains a sense of nostalgia. To enhance such a sense, the names of the medicines are also in a similar font with curved strokes.

Color

The woodcut-like colors enhance the retro sense.

Picture

Part of the drawings was blurred to enhance the image's retro look.

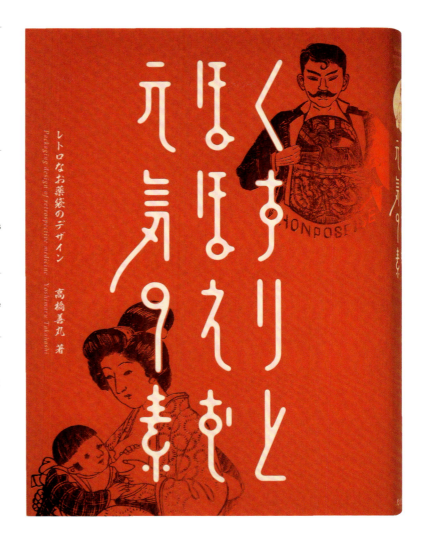

Designer: Yoshimaru Takashi

Genkinomoto Smile and Medicine (or Kusuri to Hohoemu Genki no Moto) contains Japanese drug packages from the author's collection during the 19th and 20th centuries. The collection includes many fascinating and humorous pieces. The name Genkinomoto Smile and Medicine comes from the similarity between Japanese pronunciation of "medicine" (くすり) and the sound people make when they smile (ほほえむ).

41 QUAINT POP-UP BOOK WITH MODERN CUT-AND-PASTE ILLUSTRATIONS

> ANALYSIS

Layout

The illustrations, seemingly scattered at random, are used as backgrounds to create a dazzling look.

Font

In the middle, part of the magenta gaps between the illustrations is brighter, forming Japanese characters in calligraphic style. The large characters are powerful and attractive.

Color

The magenta gaps give a vivid touch to the retro illustration that has a duller look in terms.

Picture

The cut-and-paste illustrations are creative and interesting.

Designer: Takeo Nakano

—
This is a book that introduces Tatebanko, the Japanese art of creating amazing dioramas and scenic perspectives from paper. It was popular during the Edo period.

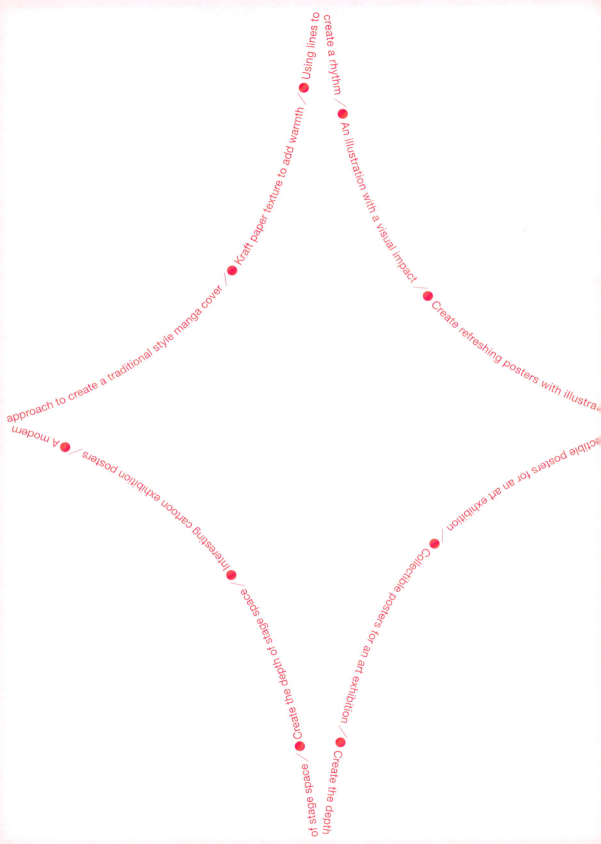

CHAPTER 5

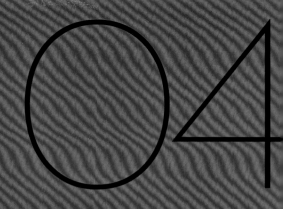

VIVIDNESS

FEMININITY AND STRENGTH PRESENTED WITH A SPECIAL COMPOSITION

> ANALYSIS

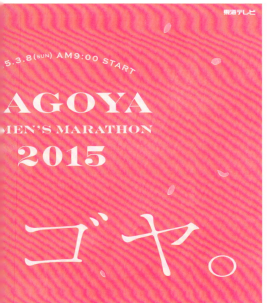

Layout

This is a rare transverse poster on which three " 女 " (the kanji for female) equally occupy one-third of the upper part while another in the same size is found at the bottom part as the first character of the title. Women run before every "female". They come across as different scenes of a race.

Font

The words are rendered in a soft font with thin strokes to match the feminine character. The English content increased this race's visibility.

Color

The main color is magenta, with sprinkles of yellow, green, reflecting feminine beauty to the competitive atmosphere.

Designer: Aya Yagi

A poster for the Nagoya Women's Marathon, the biggest women's marathon in the world.

43 COLLECTIBLE POSTERS FOR AN ART EXHIBITION

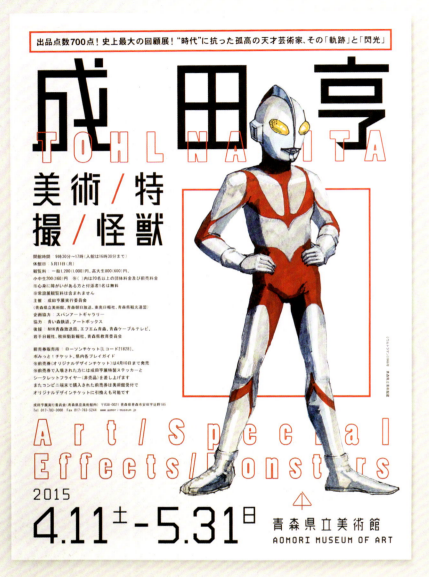

Designers: Takasuke Onishi and Jun Yamaguchi
Studio: Direction Q

—

This project introduced the achievements of the artist Toru Narita, who is well known as the designer of monster characters that are frequently seen in Japanese action movies or various TV series. The monsters grew in popularity among children when special effects were added. For the project, the exhibition of works designed and made by Toru Narita was held by Direction Q.

Layout

The poster on the left is richly layered, possessing a clear hierarchy of information. The visual subject is a hand-drawn animation character. The square behind the character increases the coherence of this poster series. The exhibition theme is efficiently conveyed through the combination of the image and main text.

Font

Both the kanji and English words utilize sans-serif fonts, enhancing the fresh and lively sense of the animation style.

Color

The limited colors seen in these posters pair well with the figures.

Picture

The posters are a collection of distinctive animation figures drawn by the artist and have a sense of theatricality.

COLLECTIBLE POSTERS FOR AN ART EXHIBITION

CREATE A SENSORY ASSOCIATION WITH THE SEA BREEZE

Designer: Sou Nomura
Studio: Studio Wonder

Uotto is an izakaya ("pub") in Hokkaido, Japan. The designer captured the lively atmosphere of the izakaya by creating a fish-like pattern for the posters. When the pattern is applied to other products in the store, it gives the impression that the fish products in the store are very fresh.

> ANALYSIS

Layout

The poster has recurring text and graphics to emphasize the main information being presented. The slightly slanted text and patterns add a bit of visual tension to it.

Font

The fishtail-like patterns are added at the end of each stroke, echoing the elements and highlighting the message of the posters.

Color

The dominant blue goes well with the seafood shop, embellished with red elements to balance the cold tone and enhance the viewer's appetite.

CREATE THE DEPTH OF STAGE SPACE

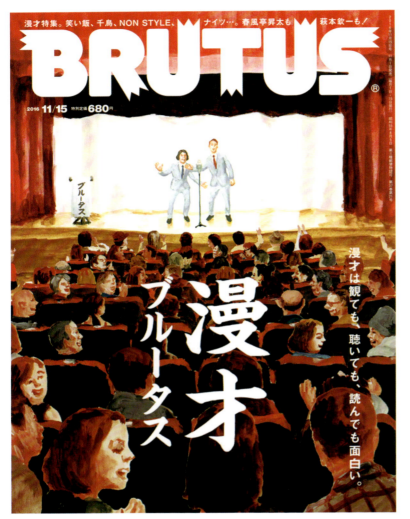

> ANALYSIS

Layout
The magazine cover is distinctive in its perspective and includes impressive depth composition with its visual tension.

Font
Viewers can understand the theme thanks to the sufficiently large text at the bottom.

Color
The warm watercolors create a fun atmosphere that is down to earth yet rich.

BRUTUS, Issue 385

—
The theme of this issue is manzai, a kind of Japanese comedy performance. It introduces the history of manzai, its performance style, and the philosophy of the humor behind it. It also includes interviews with practitioners and researchers.

INTERESTING CARTOON EXHIBITION POSTERS

150 / 151

> ANALYSIS

Layout
8 cartoons placed together make the poster look like a comic book page. Parts of the cartoon characters are placed in front of the theme text, injecting more depth and fun to the image.

Font
The font of the theme text is displayed in white boxes with black borders to separate them from the cartoon and add a layer to the poster.

Color
Though colorful and crowded, the proper proportion of white gives the poster breathing room.

Picture
Cartoon characters here are expressive, adding a dramatic vibe to the poster.

Designer: Ryu Mieno

A poster of the cartoon created by Kyuho Kotera and Shichima Sakai for the Kyoto International Manga Museum.

A MODERN APPROACH TO CREATE A TRADITIONAL STYLE MANGA COVER

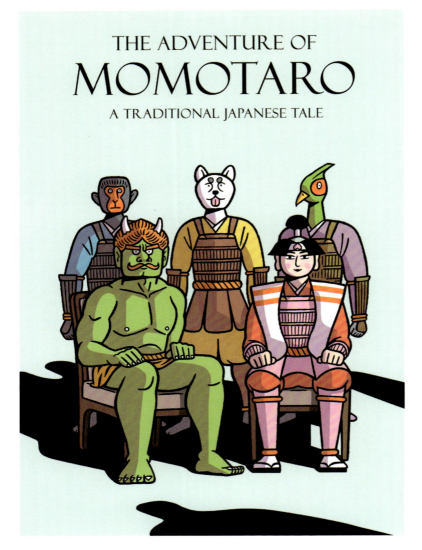

> ANALYSIS

Layout
The shadows add more depth to the cover. The shadowing done at the bottom makes the characters appear as though they are taking a group photo.

Font
The serif font adds a hint of a westernized retro vibe to this modern illustration.

Studio: Studio-Takeuma

A poster for Yuh Kamiki's US debut with his solo performance, *The Adventure of Momotaro*, which is a well-known Japanese children's folk tale.

48 KRAFT PAPER TEXTURE TO ADD WARMTH

> ANALYSIS

Layout
The cats create an interesting oval composition.

Font
The sans-serif font enhances the warm feeling.

Color
The nature tone fits the animal theme and is heartwarming.

Designer: Dyin Li

A poster for a visual project that was used in a stray cat adoption campaign. The project included a series of postcards and this poster. The illustration was inspired by the poses of the adopted cats.

49 USING LINES TO CREATE A RHYTHM

> ANALYSIS

Layout
Lines add dramatic effect and edginess to the poster, highlighting its artistic design. The theme is related to Japanese tradition, but the style aligns with current trends.

Font
The 3 big black characters read zakkado, which is a term inspired by judo, kendo, and sado. "Zakka" means sundry goods. " 道 " (Do) in Japanese means path to mastery through difficult training, so the font was designed to reflect strength and power.

Color
The bright yellow adds a modern look to the poster.

Studio: Studio-Takeuma

A poster for daily stationery goods designed by Takeuma in 2017. He is a freelance illustrator who draws in humorous style and loves animals as well as plants, he is also a frequent museum visitor as he is fascinated with mysterious cultures.

50 AN ILLUSTRATION WITH A VISUAL IMPACT

> ANALYSIS

Layout
The invisible slanted line linking the heads of the figures creates a clear and obvious sense of movement.

Font
The font feels powerful, and its color and position make it pop.

Color
The title, the most important information, is highlighted in yellow. The colors of the drawing in the background do not contrast as strongly and create a more unified look. This work has a fresh composition yet still follows the rules for creating visual layers.

TIPS: How to create visual tension?

In graphic design, tension is the sense of movement when looking at something.

We can see not only what is presented but also how each part is connected, according to Gestalt psychology. In addition, we have a desire to put things into a state of balance, such as having 2 parts in an equal proportion, a dot on the bottom of a slope. Thus, tension is formed by the conflict between the imbalance created by the arrangement of the visual elements and the subconscious desire to balance these visual elements. Creating visual tension is easy when you understand how to use these principles.

Designer: Kazumasa Tori
Studio: Studio-Takeuma

51 CREATE REFRESHING POSTERS WITH ILLUSTRATIONS

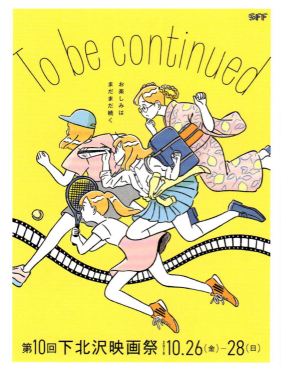
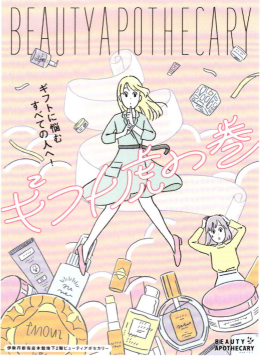

> ANALYSIS

Layout
Lively drawings to appeal to young girls.

Font
The text is organized in an orderly manner and is easy to read.

Color
The bright and lively colors cater to the target group. At the same time, the aesthetic layers and style of the illustration are enhanced.

Designer: Yuki Takahashi

Takahashi is a member of Conico. Her book *Coffee&Bread* was published by Your Mind, a Korean publisher, in 2016. The following year, her artwork collection *New Teleportation* was published by Elvis Press of Onreading, a Japanese bookstore and art gallery. Her work is frequently seen in magazines, advertisements, and CD covers.

52　ADDING A LITTLE FUN TO MAPS

漫才の聖地巡礼。

東　西

東京・浅草と大阪・なんばは東西漫才の聖地。中心となる〈浅草フランス座演芸場東洋館〉や〈なんばグランド花月〉の周辺には、幕間の休憩時間や打ち上げなど、芸人の憩いの場となり胃袋を支える店が軒を連ねる。芸人たちのエピソードなどとともに、紹介する。

東　浅草フランス座演芸場東洋館

今昔変わらず、芸人たちを支え、逸話に欠かない老舗が多数。

「たけちゃんが売れる前は、よくウチの煮込みを食べに来たんだよ」

「桂子師匠は、今も舞台終わりでふらっと来てステーキをペろり」

「ナイツの塙さんはお金がない時から、ひやしたぬきが好きでね～」

浅草六区界隈には、都内唯一のろもの寄席として多くの芸人が慕う〈浅草フランス座演芸場東洋館〉、その1階の寄席〈浅草演芸ホール〉、近隣には新人が立つ〈浅草リトルシアター〉など漫才の舞台が点在。笑いの殿堂のお膝元をぶらりと歩けば、芸人御用達の老舗がそこかしこ。溶け込み呼吸を続けている。そしてどの店主も、芸人話を振ろうものなら、ここぞとばかり逸話が飛び交うのだ。

浅草フランス座演芸場東洋館

ビートたけしの故郷とも呼ばれる演芸場。落語中心の〈浅草演芸ホール〉とともに365日休むことなく、笑いを生み出す。●東京都台東区浅草1−43−12　☎03・3841・6631。受付時間9時〜17時（公演スケジュールは月により異なるのでHPなどで確認を）。無休。

翁そば

いつの時代も安くてボリュームのあるそばを提供し続ける大正3（1914）年創業の老舗。こちらは売れる前の若手芸人の味方。ナイツ・塙さんはひやしたぬきが好きとか。●東京都台東区浅草2−5−3　☎03・3841・4641。11時45分〜15時、16時30分〜19時30分。月曜休。

ヨシカミ

「うますぎて申し訳ないス／」のキャッチコピーでも有名な浅草を代表する洋食店。ここでのステーキやビーフシチューを自腹で味わうことは、若手芸人の憧れの一つだという。●東京都台東区浅草1−41−4　☎03・3841・1802。11時45分〜22時30分。木曜休。

喫茶ブロンディ

内海桂子師匠やナイツも御用達の喫茶店。ナポリタンやハムエッグ定食、ミックスジュースまで昭和が香るメニューが充実。東洋館の目の前なので、芸人のネタ合わせや休憩の聖地。●東京都台東区浅草2−11−1　☎03・3841・1583。8時30分〜23時。無休。

珈琲アロマ

コーヒーカップに、ホーローケトルでゆっくりとネルドリップで淹れる主人渾身のコーヒーが、常に優しく迎えてくれる名喫茶。〈浅草ペリカン〉の食パンを使ったサンドも秀逸。●東京都台東区浅草1−24−5　☎03・3841・9002。8時〜18時。木曜・第4水曜休。

くじらの店 捕鯨船

ビートたけしの「浅草キッド」にも歌われるクジラ料理専門店。元浅草芸人で主人の河野過夫さんを慕う多くの芸人が通う。店の聖地にサインを書くと売れるとの験担ぎも。●東京都台東区浅草2−4−3　☎03・3844・9114。17時〜22時（土・日・祝16時〜）。木曜休。

Layout

The hand-drawn pictures are viewer-friendly, and the text is neatly arranged, making it easy to read.

Font

The neatly arranged text is easy to read.

Color

The hand-drawn pictures feel down to earth.

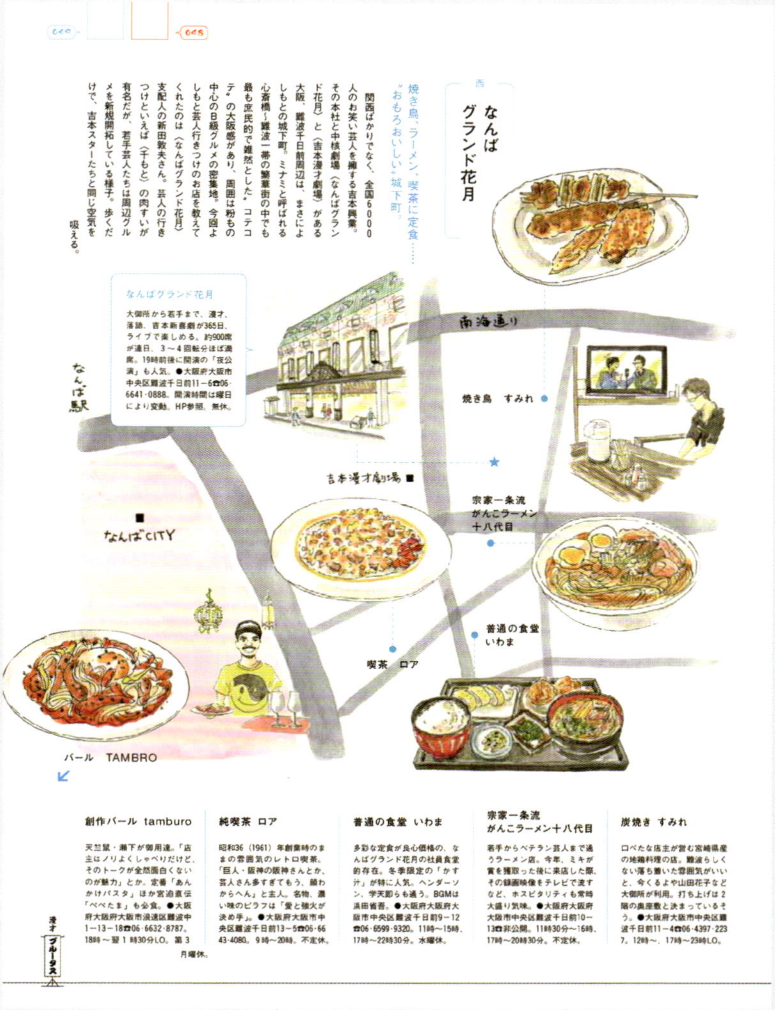

西

なんば
グランド花月

焼き鳥、ラーメン、喫茶に定食……〝おもろおいしい〟城下町。

関西ばかりでなく、全国6000人のお笑い芸人を擁する吉本興業。その本社と中核劇場〈なんばグランド花月〉と〈吉本漫才劇場〉がある大阪、難波千日前周辺は、まさによしもとの城下町。ミナミと呼ばれる心斎橋〜難波一帯の繁華街の中でも最も庶民的で雑然とした〝コテコテ〟の大阪感があり、周囲は粉もの中心のB級グルメの密集地。今回よしもと芸人行きつけのお店を教えてくれたのは〈なんばグランド花月〉支配人の新田敦夫さん。芸人の行きつけといえば〈千もと〉の肉すいが有名だが、若手芸人たちは周辺グルメを新規開拓している様子。歩くだけで、吉本スターたちと同じ空気を吸える。

なんばグランド花月

大御所から若手まで、漫才、落語、吉本新喜劇が365日、ライブで楽しめる。約900席が連日、3〜4回転分ほぼ満席。19時前後に開演の「夜公演」も人気。●大阪府大阪市中央区難波千日前11−6☎06·6641·0888。開演時間は曜日により変動。HP参照。無休。

創作バール tamburo

天竺鼠・瀬下が御用達。「店主はノリよくしゃべりだけど、そのトークが全然面白くないのが魅力」とか。定番「あんかけパスタ」ほか宮迫直伝「ぺぺたま」も必食。●大阪府大阪府大阪市浪速区難波中1−13−18☎06·6632·8787。18時〜翌1時30分LO。第3月曜休。

純喫茶 ロア

昭和36（1961）年創業時のままの雰囲気のレトロ喫茶。「巨人・阪神の阪神さんとか、芸人さん多すぎてもう、顔わからへん」と主人。名物、濃い味のピラフは「愛と強火が決め手」。●大阪府大阪市中央区難波千日前13−5☎06·6643·4080。9時〜20時。不定休。

普通の食堂 いわま

多彩な定食が良心価格の、なんばグランド花月の社員食堂的存在。冬季限定の「かす汁」が特に人気。ヘンダーソン、学天即らも通う。BGMは浜田省吾。●大阪府大阪府大阪市中央区難波千日前9−12☎06·6599·9320。11時〜15時、17時〜22時30分。水曜休。

宗家一条流 がんこラーメン十八代目

若手からベテラン芸人まで通うラーメン店。今年、ミキが賞を獲取った後に来店した際、その録画映像をテレビで流すなど、ホスピタリティも常時大盛り気味。●大阪府大阪府大阪市中央区難波千日前10−13☎非公開。11時30分〜16時、17時〜20時30分。不定休。

炭焼き すみれ

口べたな店主が営む宮崎県産の地鶏料理の店。難波らしくない落ち着いた雰囲気がいいと、今くるよや山田花子など大御所が利用。打ち上げは2階の奥座敷と決まっているそう。●大阪府大阪市中央区難波千日前11−4☎06·4397·2237。12時〜、17時〜23時LO。

漫才ブルータス

***BRUTUS*, Issue 385**

–

The theme is "Manzai's Food Tour".

● A visual focus that is instantly eye-catching ／ ● The innovative use of texture ／● A poster for a performance of an experimental music group ／ ● Colorful cross-section exhibition posters ／ ● Small and exquisite pictures as a visual guide ／ ● Posters with professional characteristics ／ ● Create attention-grabbing patterns ／ ● Bottled water that can be read ／ ● A book cover featuring the beauty of emptiness ／● Visual design that makes serious content fun ／● An animal-themed poster ／● A casual cover design with a unique font ／● Books comfy for children to read ／

CHAPTER 5

05

ORDERLINESS

A VISUAL FOCUS THAT IS INSTANTLY EYE-CATCHING

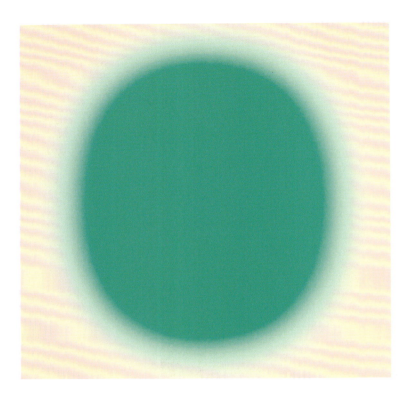

Designer: Daigo Daikoku
Studio: Daikoku Design Institute

The purpose of the poster is to emphasize Musashino Art University as a promoter of creative activities. The posters display the beauty of color.

> **ANALYSIS**

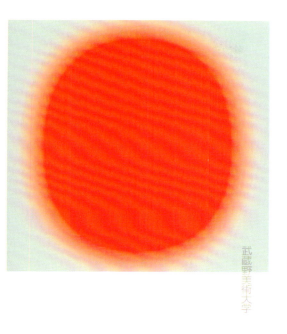
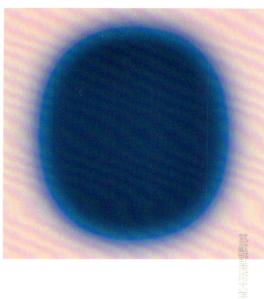

Layout

The large, blurred zone in a bright color in the middle of each poster is very eye-catching. These minimalist posters with bold colors symbolize the nature of the Musashino Art University's creativity.

Color

The blurred edges symbolize the potential of art to be diverse. The oval-shaped zones have a gradient effect at the edges that give the viewer a dreamy impression.

TIPS:

A circle, no matter how small it is when compared with other visual elements around, is always the most powerful geometric shape that can attract the eye, said Kimberly Elam in her book *Grid Systems*.

54 THE INNOVATIVE USE OF TEXTURE

> ANALYSIS

Layout

The paper-cut texture creates a strong and layered visual expression. The subtlety of the layout makes for an interesting poster. If you look closely, you can see patterns of butterflies and birds among the plants.

Font

The title appears as if it were written on the cut-out paper.

Designer: Masayoshi Kodaira

The designer's poster was an entry for the building and environment design competition sponsored by Tokyo Gasu, the biggest gas supplier in Japan. The designer's primary concern was paper and printing, rather than working on the specific design. While it was important to stick to the theme of the competition, the designer himself preferred to fuss over creating a unique font. In his opinion, there is always a font on hand that will match his idea. Therefore, he used a common font for his poster and cut out part of the text to make it look like it was written on the paper cut, which added some more dimension to the poster.

A POSTER FOR A PERFORMANCE OF AN EXPERIMENTAL MUSIC GROUP

> ANALYSIS

Layout
The left and right sides have equal space for the main visual elements. The font conveys a feeling of being primitive, simple, and bold.

Font
The characteristic tailored text is the focus of the design. The overlapped parts of the strokes that make up the text stand out. The imitation of traditional strokes written by a brush pen produces a historical and traditional look. The shape of the characters creates an impactful image.

Color
The pink background contrasts with the solid font.

Designer: Ryu Mieno

A performance by the world-famous Japanese music group Geinoh Yamashirogumi embodies a mixture of tradition and modernity. Their public performance in Bali, Indonesia was very popular.

COLORFUL CROSS-SECTION EXHIBITION POSTERS

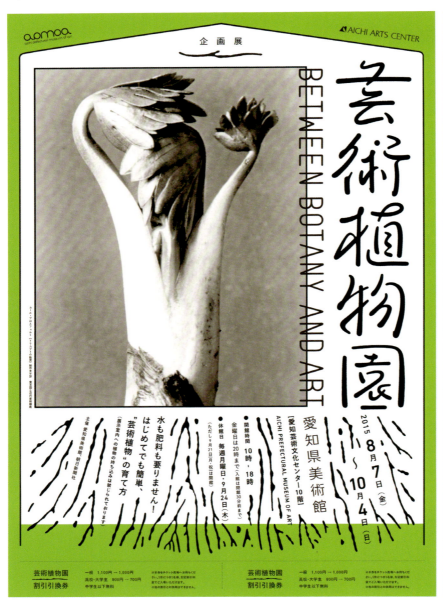
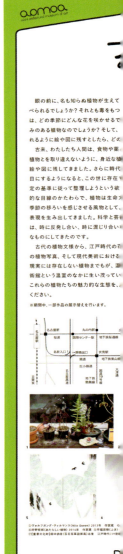

Font

The font used for the title and the patterns complement the organic lines of the plant.

Color

The lime green of the background matches the floral theme for a simple, clean, and artistic look.

Picture

The plant photo that dominates the poster on the left has its own unique beauty and provides space for individual interpretation.

Designer: Ryu Mieno

Posters for an exhibition on plants and art. It featured paintings of plants, sketches of birds, and plant specimens.

57 SMALL AND EXQUISITE PICTURES AS A VISUAL GUIDE

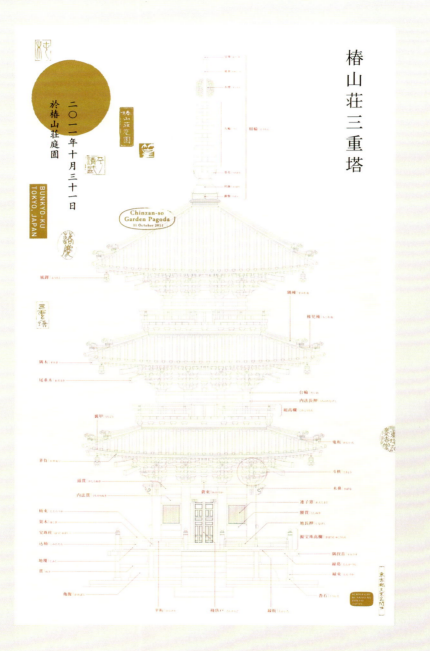

> ANALYSIS

Layout
The tour leaflets focus on the architectural features of the three-story pagoda. The small pictures serve as a visual guide and dividers for the leaflet on the right. The leaflets are elaborate for an excellent match with the traditional architectural style.

Color
Shades of brown dominate the posters, producing a peaceful and serene impression.

Designer: Daigo Daikoku
Studio: Daikoku Design Institute

—
A visual project for a Buddhist ceremony that was held when the reconstruction of the renowned Three-Story Pagoda in Chinzanso Garden was completed.

POSTERS WITH PROFESSIONAL CHARACTERISTICS

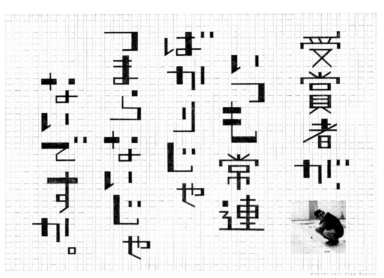
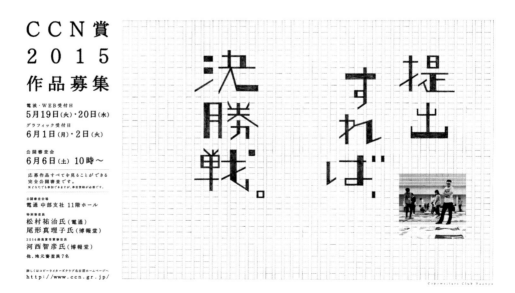

> ANALYSIS

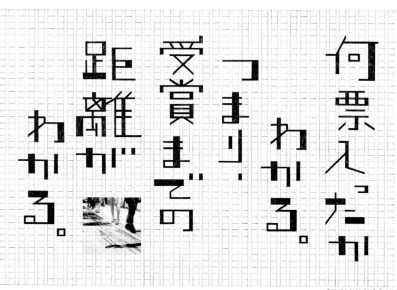

Layout

The text is done in a special font, and the typical Japanese grid paper highlights the distinguishing features of a copywriter's work.

Font

The strokes of the characters on the writing pads are mostly vertical or horizontal, running parallel to the grids. The text in the upper portion is made to look like it was written in pencil and is easy to read.

Color

The simple black and white color palette of the poster reflects the nature of a copywriter's work.

Designer: Marii Ando

—
This is the posters for the CCN Award launched by Copywriter Club Nagoya. The candidates and winners are mostly copywriters, which explains why Ando created such a characteristic font on the writing pads.

59 CREATE ATTENTION-GRABBING PATTERNS

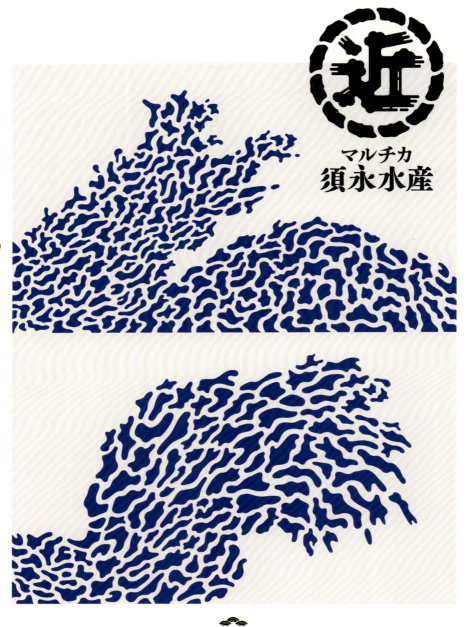

> ANALYSIS

Layout

The pattern and logo are very symbolic and prominent among the limited visual elements. The large blue patterns provide a bird's eye view of the sea.

Font

The logo is a kanji character which means "near". It is rendered in a traditional calligraphic style, but the fine details feature a very modern look.

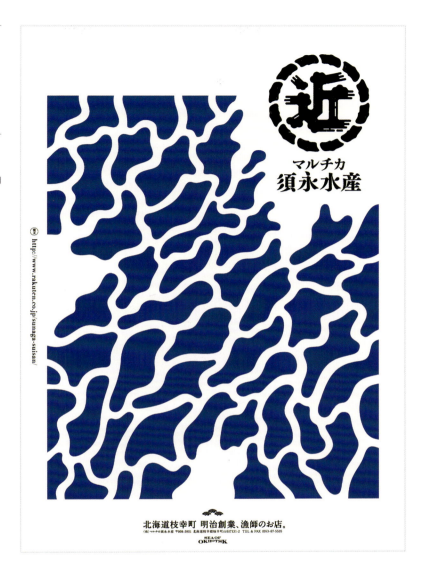

Designer: Sou Nomura
Studio: Studio Wonder

—

Sunaga Fisheries is a fishing company located in Hokkaido. Faced with increasing challenges, Sunaga Fisheries needed a new visual identity to offer customers something fresh.

CREATE ATTENTION-GRABBING PATTERNS

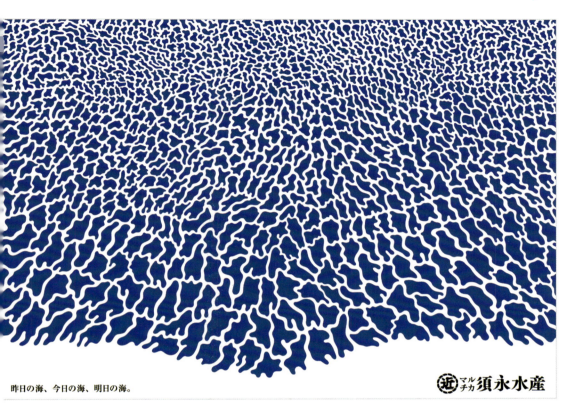

BOTTLED WATER THAT CAN BE READ

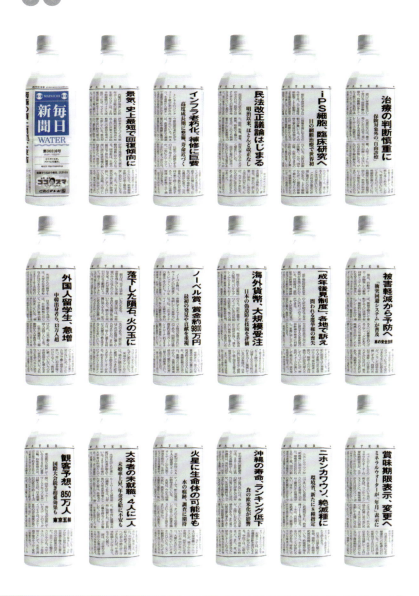

Designer: Yoshinaka Ono

31 bottled water labels with parts of real newspapers to encourage young people to read newspapers.

> ANALYSIS

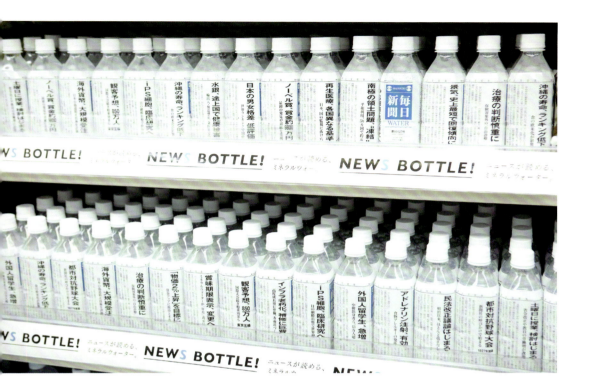

Font

The fonts on the bottles are usually used for Japanese newspapers.

Layout

A typical newspaper layout is used to create unexpected product packaging. This approach inspires designers to explore the possibilities of crossovers.

61   A BOOK COVER FEATURING THE BEAUTY OF EMPTINESS

> ANALYSIS

Layout
The subject of the book cover is a picture of a blurred light, cultivating a mysterious, uncertain, and cold aura.

Font
The title is formed by 3 words or phrases— summer, flame, and my dead body – that were done in Japanese and Chinese, the latter of which are in the boxes. The arrangement of the Chinese characters produces an uncertain and unsettled feeling, matching the theme of the novel.

Color
The book cover gives an impression of alienation with its limited colors and large area of negative space.

Picture
The abstract and blurred image symbolizes the designer's view of the book's refined imagery and stirs the viewer's imagination.

Designer: Aaron Nieh
Studio: Aron Nieh Workshop

—
The title of this book by Otsuichi creates a contrast between life and death. Nieh put such a contrast in a peaceful and clean cover to build a glass wall between the drastic contrast and the viewers. Taking place largely at night, the story conjures up the emptiness after death. When designing the cover, the designer compressed all his imagination of compulsive neatness, dead bodies, cleanness, alienation, hysterics, and floating words together and turned them into a single blank state.

古市憲寿の未来社会学

VOL.6 今月のお題：未来の保育園

SOCIOLOGY OF THE FUTURE BY NORITOSHI FURUICHI

(GO! GO! NURSERY SCHOOL!)
SHAKAIGAKUMA

それってこっちのほうがよくないですか？

イラスト・デザイン 佐野研二郎

古市憲寿 NORITOSHI FURUICHI

1985年、東京生まれ。社会学者。NHK「ニッポンのジレンマ」の司会の他、最近ではフジ系「ワイドなショー」でのクールな発言が人気。口癖は「それってどっちでもよくないですか？」。最新刊は『保育園義務教育化』(小学館)。

ノルウェーに行っていた。友だち夫婦の子どもがちょうど一歳を迎え、もうすぐ保育園に預けるというタイミングだった。

彼らはオスロという首都に住んでいるのだが、日本の待機児童問題はほとんどなく、家の近所の保育園に行くことが決まったらしい。

その保育園の説明会があったのだが、友人はすっかり待ち物の案内などがされるのだと思っていた。しかし実際にはベテラン園長による乳幼児教育の大切さを訴える講演会があった、その子の将来を考える上で非常に重要なことだ。だから保育園でも子どもがいっしょにコミュニケーション能力などの「生きる力」を身につけることがあるが、人は乳幼児期にこそ社交性や書いたことがあるが、人は乳幼児期にこそ社交性や勉強会はそんな話を熱く訴えられたという。

この夫婦は、ママだけではなくパパも保育園に子どもを通わせることに強く賛成、というか、パパ自身も4ヶ月間の育児休暇を取得していた。ノルウェーでは1歳までママとパパが交代で育児休暇を取得して、1歳からは保育園に預けるのが当たり前。いつまでも家で育児をしていると、周囲から「なんで」と不思議な目で見られたりする。

このエピソード、「さすが北欧、日本はやっぱり遅れているなあ」ということが書きたくて紹介したわけではない。実はノルウェーも戦後は、「主婦の国」と呼ばれるくらい専業主婦が多い国だったのだ。まだキリスト教系の政党は、最近まで子どもが小さいうちはママが家で育児を積極的にしたくなるような政策を打ち出していた。

そんな保守的だったノルウェーだが、今では世界に名だたる男女平等国家だ。「ジェンダーギャップ指数」という男女平等の達成度を測るランキングでは2015年で世界2位だった（ちなみに日本は101位という悲惨な結果）。

ノルウェーはなぜ変われたのだろうか？スーパーマンのような政治家が華麗な改革を断行したというわけではない。経緯は非常に地味で、まず現実が変わったのだ。男性力が足りなくなり、労働市場に多くの女性を求めた。また夫一人の稼ぎではやっていけない家が増えて、妻も働き出すようになった。こうして女性が働き始めたものの何もかもは保育園の数も、女性を支援する制度も何もかもが足りなかった。

だけど変わってしまった現実に対しては、政治も対応せざるを得ない。「遅すぎる」と批判されながら、多くの公立保育園が建てられた。また女性政治家目線で様々な制度が作られていった。

日本はまさに今、過渡期にある。現実はだいぶ変わった。女性が子どもを産んでも働き続けることはもはや当たり前。だけど制度がその現実に追いついていない。「保育園落ちた日本死ね！」というブログが話題になった時に初めて待機児童問題の深刻さに気付いた政治家も多かったという。国会議員は必ずしも広い視野を持って働いている人ばかりではない。自分の専門分野と地元の事情に詳しいかも知れないが、保育園問題なんて眼中にない人も多かった。

今年の参議院選挙から選挙権年齢が引き下げられたが、年配の政治家には「秋葉原」という貧困な想像力しか持てないくらい若者と接触がなかったようだ。

その人は、「若者＝秋葉原」と悩んでいた人もいるらしい。どんな制度も必ず現実に追いつく。そうじゃないと社会が回っていないからだ。たとえば最近注目を集めている憲法改正の議論がある。改憲派はずっとあってのだが、昔の憲論者たちは本気で天皇を日本の元首に戻し、言論の自由を制限し、男女平等を見直そうとしていた。現在の自民党の憲法改正草案にも、そのような要素は含まれている。しかしインターネットや出版

物は全て検閲します」「社会の主は男性で、女性はそれに従わなくてはいけません」というような改革が実際に通るだけで可能性は極めて低い。国内世論の大反対に違うだけではなく、国際的にも批判されるだろう。だけど同じことはもしかしたら戦後すぐだったらあり得たかも知れないし、戦前の日本は実際にそのような国だった。

一体、何が起こったのか。それは、世代交代だ。『ミライの授業』という本で紹介されていたのだが、「天動説が『常識』になったのは、天動説を信じる人が全て死んで、地動説を受け入れる人々が天動説ではなく地動説を信じる時代の中心に立った時だったというのだ。

これは、今の保育園問題にも言えることだ。「育児は母親の仕事」「子どもが3歳までは母親は家にいなくてはならない」と信じる高齢者たちは中々自分の意見を変えないだろう。しかしそのような政治家もやがて現役を引退するだろう。一方の若い政治家は、程度の差はあるだろうが、同世代が多ければ多いくらいは保育園探しに苦労しているからくらいは知っているはずだ。

だから世代交代のようなペースで、社会は必ず変わる。1年なのか、5年なのか、10年かかるのか。だけど間違いなく「未来」はもう始まっているのだ。

> ANALYSIS

Layout

The designer made serious content lively. The geometric shapes in bright colors serve as a guide for the eye. The childlike visual elements contrast with the academic language of the headline, encouraging readers to read the text.

Font

The characteristic font of the headline goes well with the geometric shapes.

Color

The toy-brick shapes serve as decoration while simultaneously sorting out the text hierarchy.

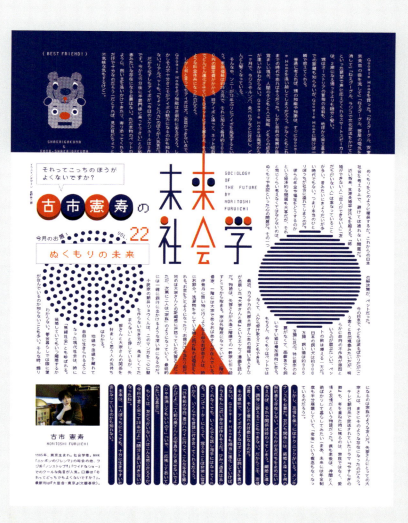

**Designers: Kenjiro Sano and Yumi Katori
Studio: Mr Design & Mr Design NY**

—

"*Sociology of the Future*" is the column by sociologist Noritoshi Furuichi in the monthly magazine VERY published by Kobunsha, in which the designer tried to create a different visual design for every theme of each month.

VISUAL DESIGN THAT MAKES SERIOUS CONTENT FUN

(LET'S STUDY!)

未来
SHAKAIGAKUMA

それってこっちのほうがよくないですか？

古市憲寿の

今月のお題：未来の教育

VOL.7

未来社会学

SOCIOLOGY OF THE FUTURE BY NORITOSHI FURUICHI

古市 憲寿
NORITOSHI FURUICHI

1985年、東京生まれ。社会学者。NHK「ニッポンのジレンマ」の司会のほか、最近ではフジ系「ワイドなショー」でのクールな発言が人気。口癖は「それってどっちでもよくないですか？」。最新刊は『保育園義務教育化』（小学館）。

イラスト・デザイン 祖父江三郎

2020年度から2022年度に日本の教育が大きく変わる。新しい学習指導要領が実施され、「ゆとり教育」にも匹敵する大改革だと言われている。

わかりやすいポイントでいうと、小学校高学年で英語が正式な教科となり、授業時間が週2コマに増加する。また小学校でプログラミング教育も必修化される予定だ。さらに、アクティブラーニングと呼ばれる議論や対話重視型の授業も全ての教科で導入されるという。

また教育改革は高等教育にも及び、大学入試センター試験も2020年1月の実施を最後に廃止され、記述式の試験も導入される予定だ。また2024年度からは、英語ではスピーキングのテストも導入される予定だ。国語と数学では、マークシートに加えて、記述式の試験をコンピューター上で解答する形になることも検討されている。

新しい学習指導要領のキーワードは「社会に開かれた教育課程」「抽象的だが、文部科学省の意向りにことが進めば、英語もプログラミングもできて、主体的に行動できる「グローバル人材」がたくさん生まれることになるようだ。

しかし課題は多い。というか、たぶんこの教育改革、絶対すぐにはうまくいかないと思う。確かにこれからの時代、英語やプログラミングができたほうがいいとは思う。

しかし断言できるのは、小学校で週2時間、英語を勉強したくらいで、それほど英語力は上達しないだろうということ。これは大人にも言えることで、週に2時間の勉強では、よほど才能がある人以外は、いつまで経っても話せない。「勉強しても英語が話せない」と言っている人の多くは、ただ単に勉強不足の場合がほとんどだ。

またプログラミングに関しては教科化が見送られ、理科や音楽の授業の中で体験的に学ばせる予定。しかし一体誰が子どもたちにプログラミングを教えるかなど問題は山積している。授業の中で少しプログラムをかじっただけで、子どもたちにとってどんな効果をもたらすかは定かではない。

な僕には、今回の教育改革が、日本のおじさんたちのコンプレックスの裏返しに思えてならない。英語も話せない、プログラミングもできない、そういった面で苦労している人が多いのではないだろうか。そのコンプレックス解消を子どもの教育に押しつけているような気がする《本当に必要だとうなら、今から自分で英語やプログラミングを勉強すればいいのに》。

このような教育改革に翻弄されるのはいつだって現場だ。何せ、これだけの教育改革なのに、現場の先生の数も予算も、あまり増やされそうもないのだ。しかし、いきなり「プログラミング」や「アクティブラーニング！」と言われても、対応できない教員も多いだろう。日本には、小中高をあわせると約100万人の先生がいる。定年間際の先生にいきなり授業スタイルを変えろと言っても難しい。

この国の初等・中等教育は国際的に見ても非常に高い水準を保っている。もっと言おう、この国の教育改革と言われるが、今の日本の教育が全然ダメなのかと疑問に思えてきるのだが、そんなことはない。たとえば、PISAという国際学習到達度調査によると、日本の15歳は世界的に見ても非常に優秀だ。

もっとも、今の教育がそのままでいいとは決して思わない。昔のように全てを暗記しなくても色々なことがネット検索でわかる時代。検索が一般的でなかった時代と今でカリキュラムがそこまで変わらないのはおかしい。

たとえば、もっと「検索」を教える授業があってもいいと思う。ただの「検索」なら子どもでもちょっとしたテクニックで、精度の高い情報を手に入れることができる。頭の悪いメディアは時々「最近の若者の心が弱いため離職率がこれだけ上がっているのだ」みたいな報道をしてしまうが、あらゆるデータは何かと比較しないと意味がない。比べないことには、その数値が高いか低いかのかもわからないからだ。

だから僕はよく、関心のあるキーワードという言葉を追加して検索をする。この場合なら「大学生 離職率 推移」といった具合に。そして直感的に理解している場合は、画像検索をする。そうすると、大学生の離職率がここ数年間、だいたい3割くらいで推移していることがわかる。

まあ、別にだれか書いたようなことを絶対に学校で教えるべきと言っているのではない。ただそんな教えられかってからでも学べるんだから。実は僕は大人になってあまり期待をしていない。なぜなら僕自身が、中学校や高校以降に習ったことに関して、ほとんど覚えていないからだ。自分では中々コントロールできないコミュニケーション能力や忍耐力を鍛える乳幼児期の教育は重要だが、それ以降の教育に過剰な必要は殆どの場合、人は結局、本当に必要なことや生活で必要になれば人は必死に覚えるし、そうでなくなれば忘れる。英語もプログラミングも仕事や生活で必要なら人は必死に覚えるし、そうでなければ忘れる。いくら教育が変わっても社会が変わらないことに意味はない。たとえば教育でいくら子どもの主体性を伸ばしたところで、本当に主体的な人物を受け入れてくれる会社が今の日本にどれくらいあるだろうか。どうせ子どもはあまり変わらないだろう。それは未来になってもあまり変わらないだろう。

古市憲寿の未来社会学

それってこっちのほうがよくないですか？

VOL.12 今月のお題：未来の肩書き

SOCIOLOGY OF THE FUTURE BY NORITOSHI FURUICHI

「将来の夢は？」

僕たちが子どもの頃から繰り返し尋ねられ、そして子どもにも尋ねてきた質問だ。男の子なら「スポーツ選手」や「警察官」、女の子なら「食べ物屋さん」や「学校の先生」というのが上位に並ぶ。

こんな夢を子どもたちが語った場合、大人たちは普通応援するフリをしてみせる。「頑張ってね」「大人になってもその夢をなくさないでね」とか言ったりして。

しかし、ほとんどの子どもはこの夢は叶えることはない。「スポーツ選手になれる可能性は非常に低いし、逆に「食べ物屋さん」は高校生にもなれば一番気軽にできるバイトの一つで、夢でも何でもなくなる。

加えて、「将来の夢」を聞く大人が見過ごしていることがある。それは子どもが夢を叶えることはなく、2030年代から2040年代は、現代では存在していない仕事もあるだろうし、新しく生まれている職業もあるだろう。その時には消えている仕事もあるだろうし、2017年の価値観で、子どもの未来を規定する必要は必ずしもないのだ。

キングコングの西野亮廣さんも、ブログでこんなことを書いていた。大人たちは、若者が将来の夢を持っていないことを嘆く。しかし「やりたいことが見つからない」というのが、「今の時代に合った、一番正しい答えだ、と。

西野さんはこう言う。肩書きには何の価値もない。問題なのは「何者であるかよりも「何ができ

るか」だと。確かにそうだと思う。

僕も、「社会学者」という肩書きに関してバッシングを受けることがあるが、彼らは大学業務や学生指導の大変さを理由に挙げながら、メディア出演や人狼など、毎日そこそこ忙しい。

肩書きが意味を持たなくなる時代、子どもにとるんな「夢」を言ってもらえばいいのだろうか、と。西野さんは、一つは、専門性を持つことだと思う。たとえば、お笑いという専門があり、その時点で評価されていたから、絵本作家としても注目されやすかった。

現に彼は素晴らしい絵本を書いている。狂気しか感じないエピソードだが、逆に「いつか素晴らしい小説を書くんだ」と妄想しながら、どこにも作品を投稿しない人が大成する可能性はほぼゼロで、今や「小説家になろう」など小説投稿サイトがたくさんあるのだから、どんどん作品を発表してトライ＆エラーを繰り返せばいい。そして自分に才能がなければ、すぐに違う夢を追えばいい。要は「自分が自然にしてしまうこと」「ストレスなくできることの中で、社会からも評価を得られる専門性を探すのが大事だということだ。

そして専門性は、できれば複数あったほうがいい。というか、「そこそこの能力」でも、それが二つ以上組み合わさると「なかなかの才能」になる。僕は難しいことを考える能力と、文章の上手な人は山ほどいる。でも、学者の議論をわかりやすく紹介できるという意味で学者としては凡庸だと思うし、ライバルはあまりいない。

才能とは、社会の中で一定の評価を受け、自分がそれほどストレスなくできることを見つけていく過程で開発するものなのだと思う。

これからの時代、専門性に加えて宣伝になるのは経験だ。あるNHKの討論番組に出た時のことである。「みなさまのNHK」らしく、スタジオには文化人や経済人のゲストの他に、「市民のみなさん」が100名ほど集められていた。テーマは長時間労働

ったのだが、面白かったのは「市民のみなさん」のほうが評論家のようなことを言い、ゲストは自分の体験談ばかりを話していたことだ。

たとえば「市民の新自主義が進む中で、非正規雇用が増えた」の意見。一方で経済界からのゲストは「我が社」の話をしたりするだけなので、いわば体験している国の会議の知識を話したりするだけなので、いわば体験談だ。要は、ゲストたちは特殊な世界で活動しているので、自分の経験がそのまま市民価値を持ち話になってしまうのである。

インターネットのある時代、ちょっと検索すれば誰だって経済や政治について語ることができる。人間は17時間起きていると、胎町状態の時と同じパフォーマンスになる。だから長時間労働は企業にとっても効率が悪い」とかね。

どうだ、そんな話をわざわざ「専門家」にしてもらう必要がない。というか、そんな検索で済む話しかできない「専門家」はもはや必要ない。

「肩書きに何の価値もない」という発言だから説得力がある。芸人としても絵本作家としても成功した西野さんだから脱帽できても、「ふーん」と言われて終わりだろう。確かにそうだろうね。

こう考えると、結局「肩書き」にも意味があるという。そしてこの社会で、最も手軽に手に入る肩書きは学歴だ。お笑い芸人や絵本作家として成功するよりも有名大学に入るのは遥かに簡単。夢がないという子は、普通に勉強させましょう。

古市憲寿
NORITOSHI FURUICHI

1985年、東京生まれ。社会学者。NHK「ニッポンのジレンマ」司会。他、最近ではフジ系「ワイドなショー」でクールな発言が人気。口癖は「それってどっちでもよくないですか？」。最新刊は『保育園義務教育化』（小学館）。

63 AN ANIMAL-THEMED POSTER

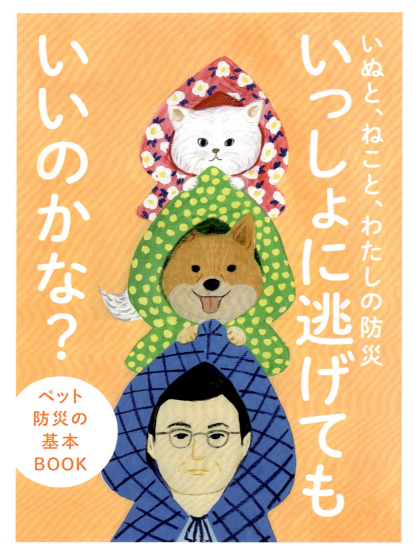

> ANALYSIS

Layout
Words are aligned vertically. The drawing gives viewers a warm, cozy feeling.

Font
The sans-serif font with curved strokes goes well with the drawing. The concise words convey the important information very effectively.

Color
Magenta, cyan, and blue symbolize freedom and vibrancy, while the magenta and green are contrasting colors, creating an eye-catching look.

Designer: Go Takahashi

The man and the animals are in a kerchief. This kind of kerchiefs is frequently worn by traditional Japanese on Japanese TV or film when they fled to safety, though they were also worn on many other occasions. Using such imagery, the designer communicated that the exhibition was for the protection of pets during disasters. During the exhibition, visitors could learn about how pet owners and non-pet owners feel and hear ideas and suggestions from local authorities and non-pet owners.

A CASUAL COVER DESIGN WITH A UNIQUE FONT

> ANALYSIS

Layout

Kazunari Hattori, the designer, thought outside of the box when designing the layout. The words seem to be written casually yet share a fixed style.

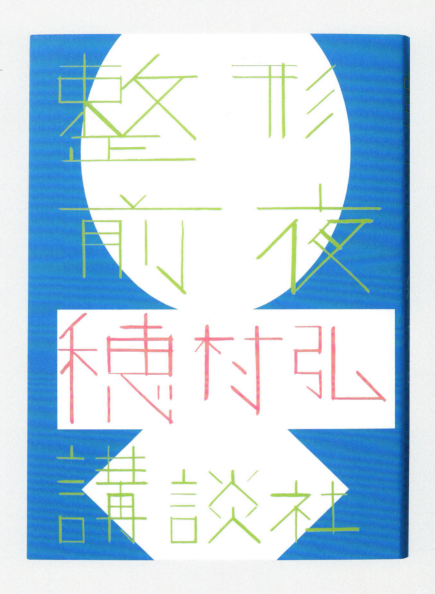

Designer: Kazunari Hattori

A book cover designed by Kazunari Hattori.

BOOKS COMFY FOR CHILDREN TO READ

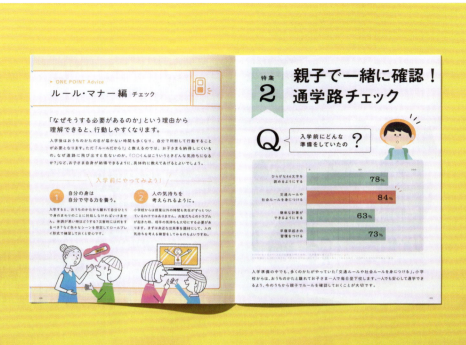

> ANALYSIS

Layout

The pages are lively and fresh with distinctive themes. They fit children's reading habits. The information hierarchy is clear.

Color

The pages feature bright colors and cute figures

Designer: Atsushi Ishiguro

Children's book published by Benesse Corporation. Atsushi Ishiguro designed the year-round educational tools for the company.

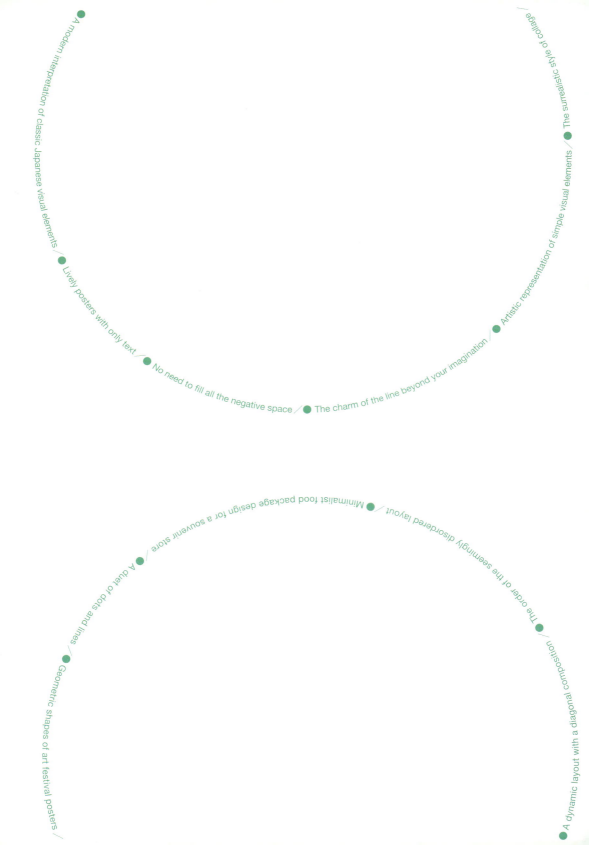

CHAPTER 5

GEOMETRIC SHAPES

66 A MODERN INTERPRETATION OF CLASSIC JAPANESE VISUAL ELEMENTS

Designer: Vitor Manduch

The designer was interested in Japanese culture and incorporated the Japanese flag into this project. He created this series of posters for his favorite Japanese bands and music.

> ANALYSIS

Layout

The big circle in each poster makes it look like the national flag of Japan, giving the posters a distinctly Japanese look.

Font

Sans-serif font provides a simple reading experience.

Color

The colors are refined and minimal.

A MODERN INTERPRETATION OF CLASSIC JAPANESE VISUAL ELEMENTS

67 LIVELY POSTERS WITH ONLY TEXT

昨年の夏、突如東京に現れた恐竜たちが、
大阪に引き続き、名古屋の「ON READING」、「KAKUOZAN LARDER」に大集合！
17名の作家が創り出す恐竜の世界をお楽しみください。
作家数やグッズ等もボリュームアップしてお待ちしております。

〈出展作家〉
ancco ／ いでたつひろ ／ オカタオカ ／ 大河原健太郎
オオクボリュウ ／ OLGA -goosecandle- ／ 岡村優太
加瀬透 ／ 片岡メリヤス ／ 鈴木哲生 ／ DAISAK
ちえちひろ ／ てんしんくん ／ まつのあやか
西雄大 ／ ヌトグラン ／ 紅 林 Hori b. Goode

大恐竜博
DINOSAUR EXPO

DINOSAUR EXPO 大恐竜博 3.30-4.11
ON READING KAKUOZAN LARDER

2016年3月30日(水)‒4月11日(月)
※KAKUOZAN LARDERは3月31日(木)より

ON READING
名古屋市千種区東山通5-19
カメダビル2A
TEL：052-789-0855
OPEN：12:00〜20:00
定休日：火曜日
http://www.onreading.jp

KAKUOZAN LARDER
名古屋市千種区覚王山通9-14
TEL：052-762-2786
OPEN：11:45〜22:00(L.O. 21:00)
定休日：火曜日・第1&3水曜日
https://m.facebook.com/KakuozanLarder

※ご来店の際は1オーダーお願いします。

> ANALYSIS

Layout

The curved lines and words aligned with other visible or invisible curved lines create an abstract flowing effect.

Color

The combination of red and white is a classic color combo in Japan.

Designer: Toru Kase

The Dinosaur Expo, held in Tokyo, Osaka, and Nagoya, was a collection of works from many illustrators and designers. For the 1st exhibition in Tokyo, the designers arranged the text as dinosaur bones that were scattered about randomly. The text has a special layout that communicates the essential information, which also serves as the entire visual design framework. For the 2nd exhibition in Osaka, a new visual design was used. The visual design in Osaka was more abstract than what was used in Tokyo. The 3rd exhibition was in Nagoya, where the visual design presentation was the most abstract of the 3.

NO NEED TO FILL ALL THE NEGATIVE SPACE

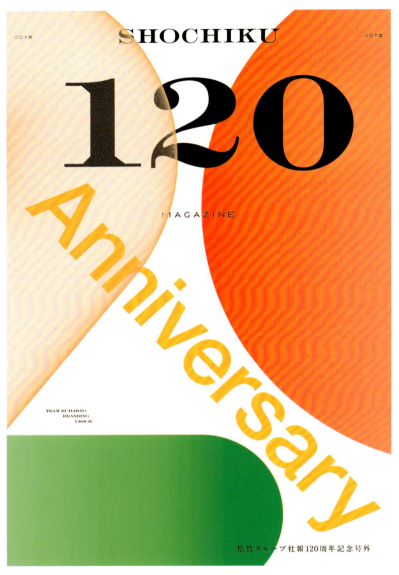

Designer: Motoi Shito

Shochiku Magazine Extra is an issue published by Matsutake Corporation to commemorate the 120th anniversary of its founding. The initial "S" of "Shochiku" (which stands for pine and bamboo, both considered noble plants in Japanese culture) is used as a motif on the right cover to represent a positive outlook toward the future.

> ANALYSIS

Layout

The main colors of the poster extend from the corners. Together, they create a balance and highlight the main text by surrounding it. The translucent color areas and the negative space result in a transparent look. The words link every part of the negative space to enhance the wholeness of the posters.

Font

The mix of modern fonts and classic serif fonts is brilliant, and the words are concise.

Color

The colors are simple, exquisite, and delightful.

THE CHARM OF THE LINE BEYOND YOUR IMAGINATION

> ANALYSIS

Layout

The patterns are like a projection of a scene in which music, graphics, and imagery merge. The geometric shapes presented in different colors are multi-layered and full of much rhythm.

Font

The theme "This Week" is done in a very stylish font. The cubist-style geometric shapes are also created based on the theme words.

Color

The retro vibe of the colors invites viewers to imagine the music project.

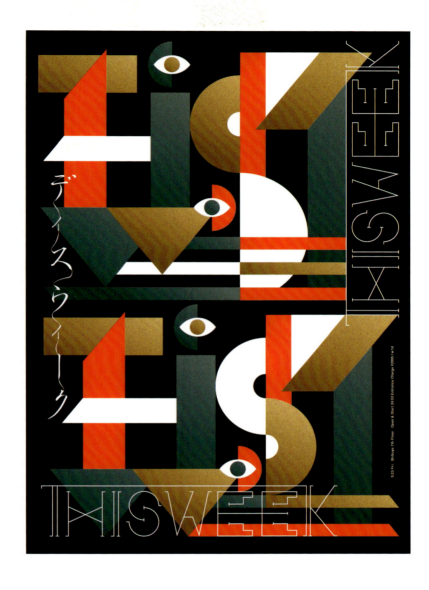

Designer: Motoi Shito

—
A poster for This Week, a DJ music project.

70 ARTISTIC REPRESENTATION OF SIMPLE VISUAL ELEMENTS

> ANALYSIS

Layout

The multi-layered arrangement of the simple visual elements represents the passion and occasionally calm introspection of 20th-century avant-garde artworks. It utilizes many graphic elements from that era.

Color

Blue, orange, and green give a vivid touch to the background in soft salmon.

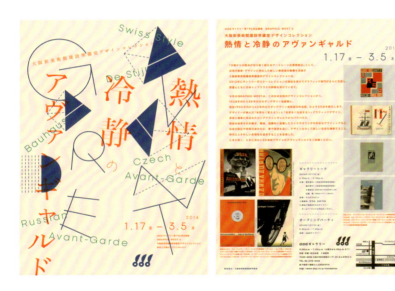

Designer: Satoshi Kondo
Studio: Asatte Design Office

—

Posters for Graphic West 6: Museum of Modern Art Osaka exhibition. The museum, which has been officially renamed Nakanoshima Museum of Art, Osaka, exhibits contemporary art and design. The artworks in the new museum are among the most important collections in Japan, both in terms of quantity and quality. The series of works on display focused on the modern design from its emergence in the 1920s to its maturity after WWII.

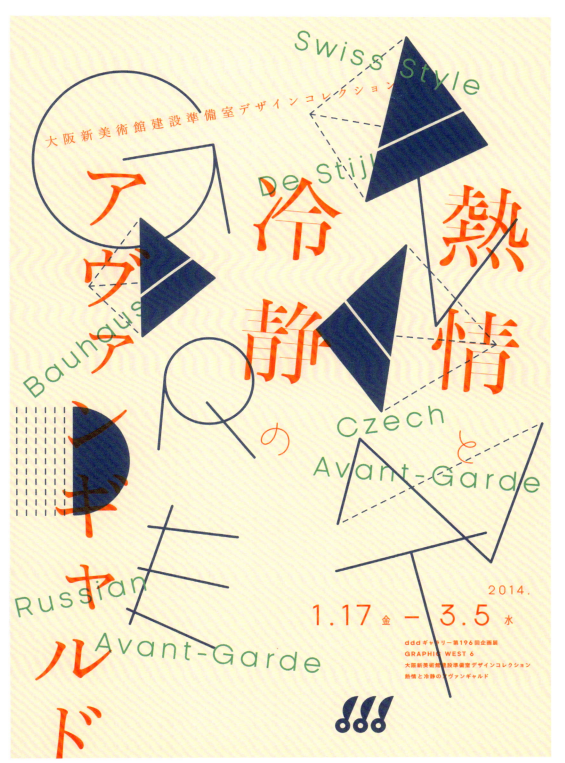

•71 THE SURREALISTIC STYLE OF COLLAGE

> ANALYSIS

Layout
The poster gives a fantastical and psychedelic feeling. The real-life photo and the drawing of 2 people kissing or biting something seem completely disconnected, yet the yellow pattern creates an interesting and mysterious connection between them.

Color
The drawing of the poster in white, blue, and red creates a rather strong contrast to the warm brown background.

idea, Issue 374

This issue contains an interview with Kenichi Samura, a long-time collaborator of the famous Japanese director Juzo Itami. The interview covered the design process and stories behind the films and the classic posters designed by the designer.

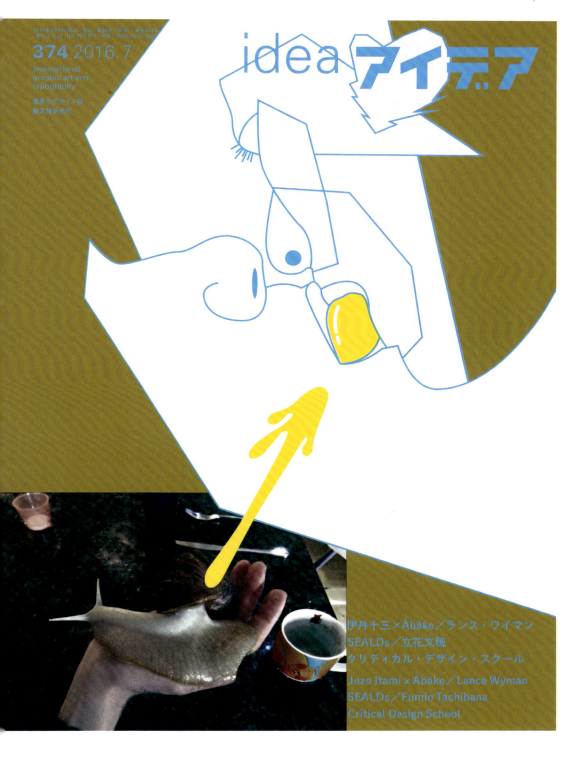

72 A DYNAMIC LAYOUT WITH A DIAGONAL COMPOSITION

> ANALYSIS

Layout
The flying bird across the diagonal line of the background imparts a sense of vigor.

Font
The text aligned with the curve of the bird's tail increases the image's dynamic look.

Color
The orange background symbolizes vigor and hope.

Designer: Toru Kase

Posters of an exhibition of final year projects of Kuwasawa Design School. Toru Kase designed the posters based on the wish that students could fly high to where they wanted to arrive.

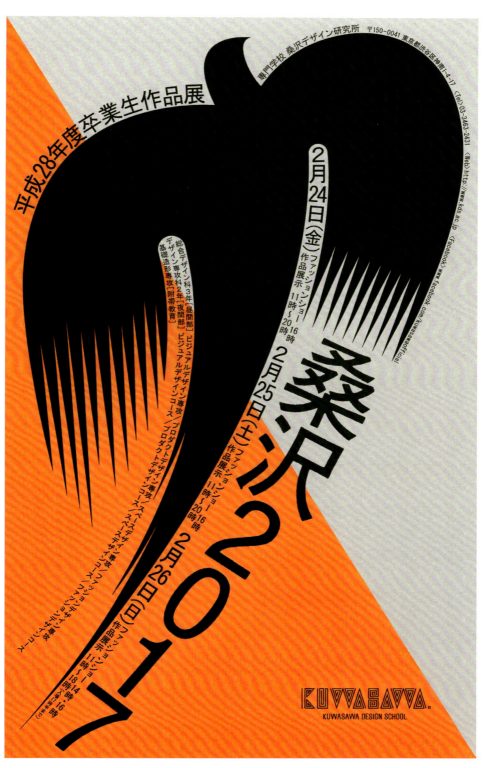

73 THE ORDER OF THE SEEMINGLY DISORDERED LAYOUT

> ANALYSIS

Layout

The designer of this poster uses a seemingly random pattern to layout George Nelson's name, but in fact the pattern fits our reading habits. Scattered profiles of his works can be seen, such as the Ball Clock and Coconut Chai. The overall layout is fascinating and has its own kind of rhythm.

Color

Red and white is a common color pairing in Japan. The designer turned white to beige to give the posters a touch of vintage.

Picture

The monochromic pictures of Nelson in red and black go well with the design's patterns.

Designers: Takeo Nakano, Kaoruko Naoi, and Ami Kawase
Studio: Nakano Design Office Co., Ltd

Posters of an exhibition of George Nelson, the industrial designer, in Meguro Museum of Art.

MINIMALIST FOOD PACKAGE DESIGN FOR A SOUVENIR STORE

Designer: Manabu Mizuno
Studio: Good Design Company

—

Packages of foods provided by a concept store in Kyoto, Japan, which combined Japanese technology, art, artifacts, and food.

> ANALYSIS

Layout
Limited visual elements highlight product features.

Font
The traditional fonts, some in a block print style and some done in calligraphy, imply that these are traditional foods.

Color
Though minimalist and clean, a touch of warm color whets viewers' appetites.

MINIMALIST FOOD PACKAGE DESIGN FOR A SOUVENIR STORE

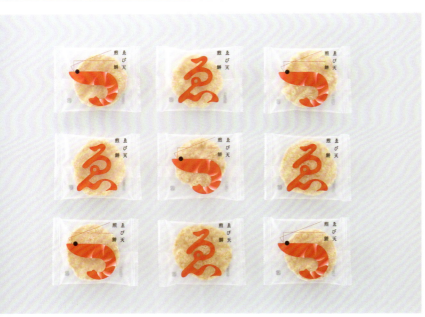

75 A DUET OF DOTS AND LINES

Designer: Atsushi Ishiguro

Posters for the exhibition Dot Trip. Movies, music, and artworks can inspire designers, but Atsushi Ishiguro, who is a fan of cooking, usually gets inspiration from tasty food, tableware, and the arrangement of those elements.

> ANALYSIS

Layout

The dense dots before and behind the lines or trunks are rhythmic, producing a vivid impression, despite the posters being done in cold dots. Graphic design featuring geometric shapes never goes out of fashion. While some dots were printed, some were carved out. These holes break through the boundary of 2-dimensional graphic design.

Color

The black dots and round holes create an interesting contrast and add additional layers to the posters.

A DUET OF DOTS AND LINES

GEOMETRIC SHAPES OF ART FESTIVAL POSTERS

Designers: Masashi Murakami and Moe Shibata
Studio: Emuni

Posters for Tokyo Festival 2017 organized by the Tokyo Metropolitan Government. Murakami and Shibata were in charge of the artistic direction of the promotional materials of the festival for that year, including a new logo that featured a spotlight illuminating a stage. The logo was seen in various print materials.

> ANALYSIS

Layout

The shapes spotlights with a beam at a place dominate the posters. This spotlight-like shape is the logo of Tokyo Festival 2017. With these shapes, the designer sought to convey the idea that art enlightens the world. Key information is also embedded in these shapes.

Font

Words in the sans-serif fonts are uncluttered and strong.

Color

The dominant magenta and jungle green create a contrast between cold and warm colors.

Picture

In order to maintain the overall visual effect, pictures were cut, or the backgrounds were removed.

TIPS:

Diagonal composition adds dynamics to a picture, painting, or poster.

Balanced composition: 2 parts in a frame are in equal proportion, making them dull and unattractive.

Diagonal composition: It conveys change and produces a sense of movement.

GEOMETRIC SHAPES OF ART FESTIVAL POSTERS

●CHAPTER

Quick Overview of the Layouts in This Book

- Key information
- Main supporting information
- Other supporting information
- Images/patterns

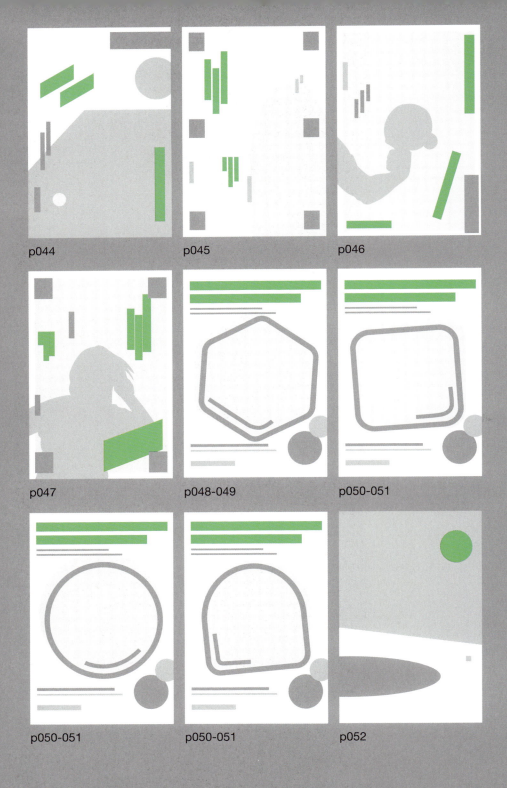

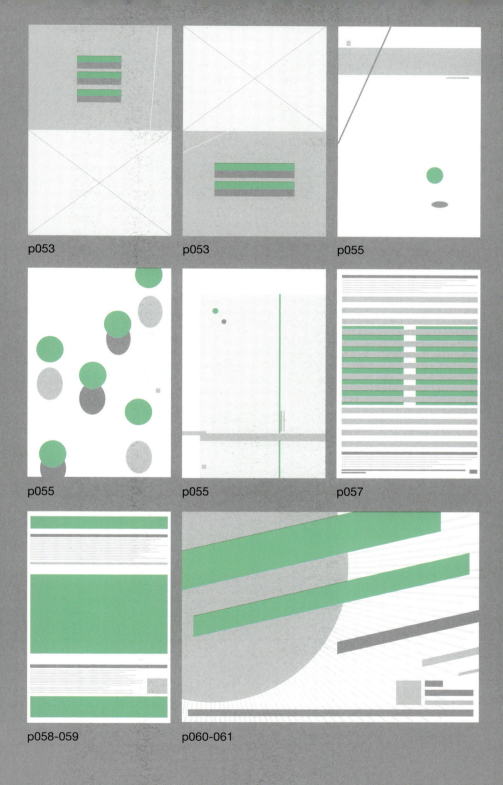

p053 p053 p055

p055 p055 p057

p058-059 p060-061

p060-061

p062

p063

p063

p064-065

p066

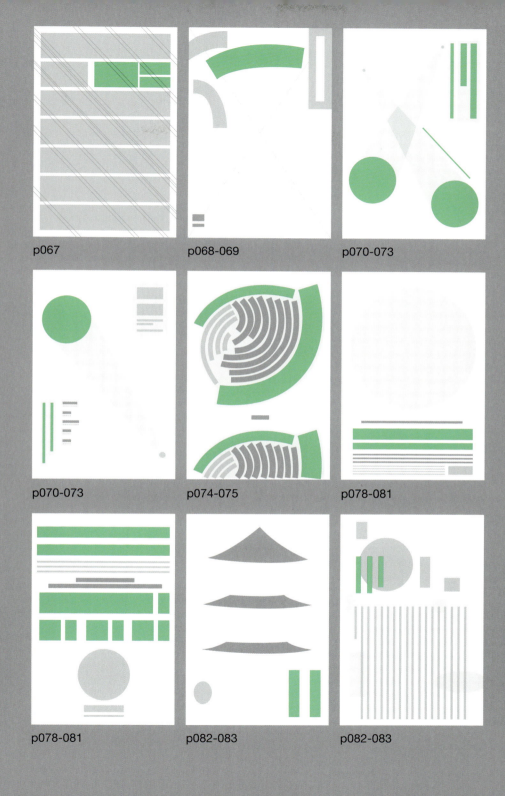

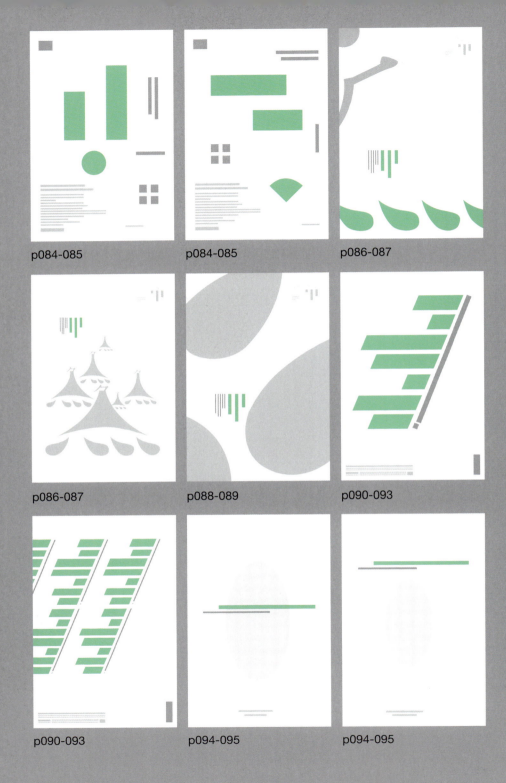

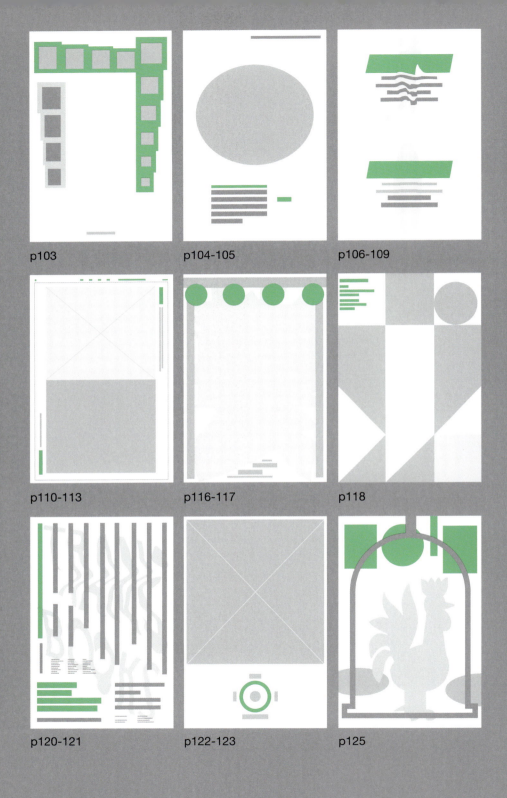

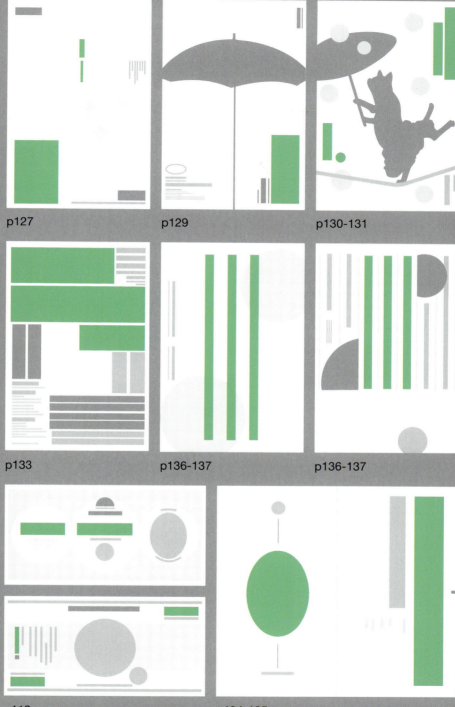

p127

p129

p130-131

p133

p136-137

p136-137

p119

p134-135

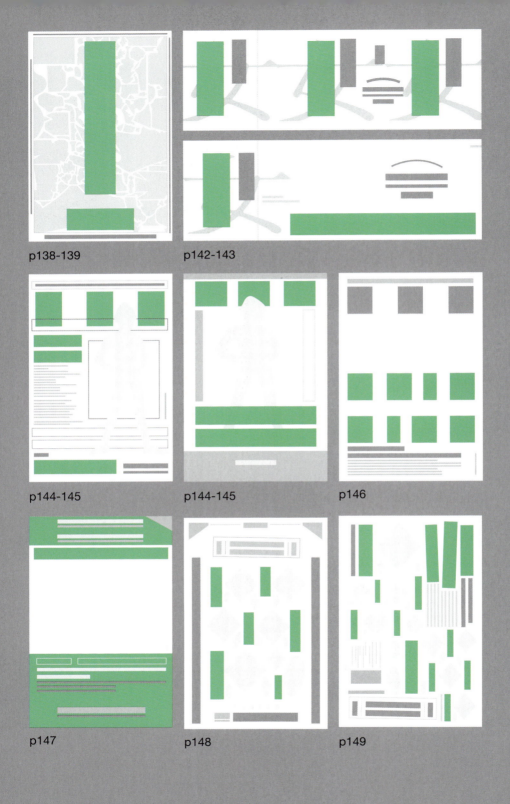

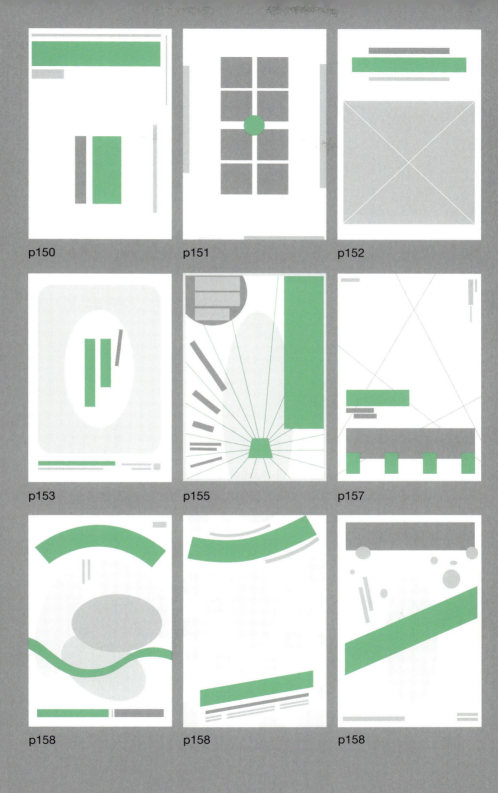

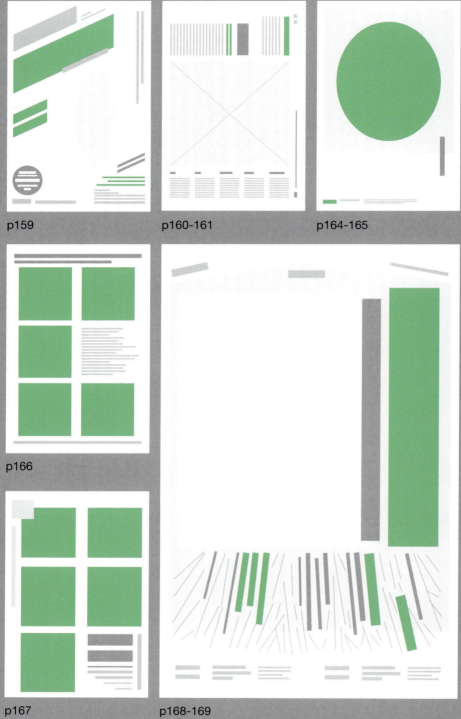

p159

p160-161

p164-165

p166

p167

p168-169

p168-169

p170-171

p170-171

p172-173

p174-177

p174-177

p174-177

p178-179

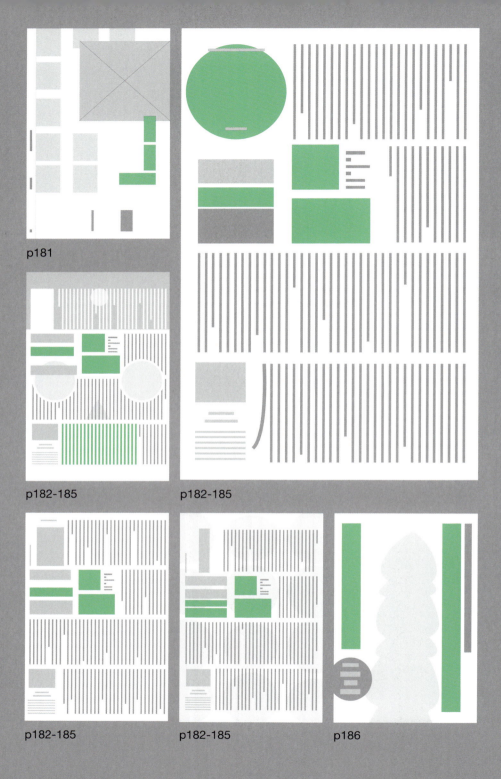

p181

p182-185

p182-185

p182-185

p182-185

p186

p214-217

p214-217

p214-217

p218-221

p218-221

p218-221

Acknowledgements

We would like to thank all the designers and contributors who have been involved in the production of this book. Their contributions have been indispensable to its creation. We would also like to express our gratitude to all the producers for their invaluable opinions and assistance throughout this project. And to the many others whose names are not credited but have made specific input in this book, we thank you for your continuous support.

Future Cooperations

If you wish to participate in SendPoints' future projects and publications, please send your website or portfolio to **editor02@sendpoints.cn**